MW00606643

All the best!
Patricia Chase Allen

HANDS IN THE EARTH

Patricia Chase Allen

Copyright © July 2010 by Patricia Chase Allen
All rights reserved
No part of this publication may be reproduced in whole or in part,
or stored in a retrieval system, or transmitted in any form or by any
means, electronic, mechanical, photocopying, recording or
otherwise, without written permission of the author.

Hands In the Earth by Patricia Chase Allen

ISBN: 978-1-4507-2469-2

Childhood Memoir
Young Readers
Farm Life
1950's Vermont
Vermont Nostalgia

Publisher: Book in Hand Publishers

Printed in the United States of America
by Print Tech, Burlington, VT

Cover design: Futura Design.

Cover photograph: Harriet M. Chase

Back cover photo: Lynn Schouten

This book is typeset using Bookman Old Style

An instructional guide is
available for teachers and parents.

Patricia Chase Allen, Author
Phone: 802 - 864 - 9799
Pictallen@aol.com
www.bookinhandpublishers.com

This memoir is dedicated to Sandy,
the other little kid, and to Dad,
the late Raymond E. Chase.

*****

*There, that task is finished. Now we can
move on to other jobs that need to be done.*
My father, Raymond E. Chase

ACKNOWLEDGEMENTS

Any task, begun in earnest for the first time, requires assistance from many people, family and friends alike. I have many to thank. Thanks to my sister, Harriet M. Chase, and family friend Ronald Sanford I have collected copies of historic photographs and other documents useful in writing this book. I thank other family members who read parts of *Hands in the Earth* and offered their input.

Many people offered to read selections and gave me valuable information to put together a historical story for schoolchildren. Their contributions have been most welcome and helped me to improve my storytelling ability. Flora Chicoine, once a Vermont farm girl herself, read my manuscript early on and offered great reviews that encouraged me to stay on track. Jeanne Lynch, Barbara Heeter, Jean Nekola, and Joan Matthews, all friends, read parts or all of my manuscript and offered friendly advice. In particular, I owe a debt of gratitude to Linda Ayer for her editing skills. She laboriously read through every chapter and seemed as energetic about my manuscript as I.

As a member of Women of UVM, I was fortunate to join a Life History Journaling Group. I'd like to thank Pat Allen Morgan for extending some of her profound writing skills on to me. Other members of the group did the same, offering encouragement and suggestions.

My brother-in-law, Win Tandy, and Errol Beach, computer experts, taught me skills here in front of my computer. I thank both of these men for passing on some of their wizardry to me.

Many of my family members and friends have been important to me in my journey into the past.

Contents

INTRODUCTION

*If you can learn a simple trick, you'll get along a lot better
with all kinds of folks. You never really understand a person
until you consider his point of view.*
Harper Lee

What would you do if you were offered a job, your very first one, at the age of eleven? How would you react? If you're anything like me, you'd gloat with pride, excitement, and near-conceit. That's how Sandy and I reacted. Sandy was just nine and her behavior at any kind of excitement was demonstrated by dancing and twisting from side to side as if she had taken center stage at Chandler Music Hall, Randolph's showcase for the arts.

She held my hands and shouted, "Pat, come let's dance! Patty! We've got a job! Come on, dance! We're going to earn lots of money. Dance with me! Dance!"

I could not muster up her kind of excitement best shown by her movement. While I was enthusiastic about the job, complete with butterflies in my stomach, I could not dance as she often did when excited about any new endeavor. She exuded happiness through her dance-like movements.

Sandy and I, the youngest in a family of seven chil-

Mother, Sandy, Harriet, Carolyn, me, Dad, and brothers Clarence, Gene, and Raymond standing, 1946

dren, and my two older sisters had been hired as well. Harriet was almost fourteen and Carolyn was twelve. When compared to them, they often seemed grown up and mature but not Sandy and me. We were pegged as the "little kids" and it seemed as if we'd remain that way forever, frozen in time at nine and eleven.

The four of us accepted the job offer with relish; we harbored no doubt that we could do the work. After all, all of us Chase kids were known for our work ethic and reliability.

The year was 1954; now generations have gone by. I was happy with the prospect of earning real money working for the State of Vermont at the Vermont School of Agriculture. The VSA was located about a mile from our family farm. We Chase girls were about to help harvest and process the summer strawberry crop.

There was an odd problem to overcome, however, before we could begin. We girls had spent years helping with all kinds of chores and tasks that needed to be done on our family farm. But in order to get a job we needed Social Security cards!

Together the four of us had filled out the forms at the local post office, sent them in the mail to the Social Security office, and we waited every day for their arrival in the mail. We were ready and raring to go!

There were many chores that needed to be completed on a dairy and vegetable farm. First, our animals needed care every day. Our cattle, calves, and pigs needed food, water, and exercise, as well as a clean and warm place to live during the cold winter. Our cows needed to be brought from our pastureland into the barn for their twice-a-day milking during the warmer seasons. Our crops needed attention throughout the planting, growing, and harvesting season. And, we hadn't needed any kind of card to work with our dad.

Life in the 1950s was very different from the way most of us experience our lives today. Our family, for example, did not own a television nor did we have computers, cell phones, or video games. There were no printers at home, no internet or Web sites to explore and no DVDs or CDs. Blackberries and ipods were not available. Television was new in our state and very few families in Randolph owned one. Our major links to the world were radios, newspapers, books, magazines, and movies.

On the other hand, there were many similarities with life today. For example we attended school; we loved books, movies, comics, and animals. We enjoyed socializing with our friends as well as our family. My family was large and yours may be also. And you may live on a farm, too. We got along well considering the number of us and the differences in our personalities. Too, we had many squabbles.

My father loved Vermont in many of the same ways as Calvin Coolidge, a Vermont-born president. "Vermont is a state I love," explained President Coolidge when he visited Vermont following the devastating 1927 flood from which Vermonters were recovering. Bridges, roads, dams, homes, farm animals, and businesses had been washed away.

News reporters stated that Vermont had lost one hundred years of progress because of the flood's damage. However, less than a year later, railroad lines had been restored. Highways, homes, and farms had been rebuilt or repaired. Dams and bridges were back in place and businesses were recovering from their losses. President Coolidge was proud of the way Vermonters had worked to recover from the flood.

Known as "Silent Cal," President Coolidge had a repu-

Damaged bridge entering Randolph after the Flood of 1927

tation for saying very little. Press releases warned that he would give no speeches on his Vermont train tour in September 1928. That was all right with Vermonters; they only yearned to see him before he left office. My dad, a young man at the time, liked President Coolidge.

The President's train had traveled north making many stops along its way. In Burlington, the train moved toward the south and again stopped at towns along its route. The final whistle stop was in Bennington.

Autumn is the time of year when our hills are aflame with fall foliage. The leaves, with colors of deep reds, oranges, and yellows of many differing shades, develop beautiful sights. Add to the scenery blue skies with billowing white clouds, deep green conifers, ripening hues

Autumn beauty in Vermont

of Vermont's abundant crops, crystal blue lakes, and pretty wildflowers dotting the countryside-all helped in the creation of a rainbow of colors.

At each community, the President had stood at the rear of the train's platform waving politely to well-wishers who came to see him. As planned, he had not spoken, not a word.

However, his reaction to well-wishers in Bennington was vastly different when he sighted a charming child. The American Legion Band played lively music. Schoolchildren carrying small American flags waved and clapped their greetings. A young girl handed the President her tiny flag. As the President received it, he stood tall and straight, and with deep emotion began to speak.

"I love Vermont because of her hills and valleys, her scenery, and her invigorating climate; but most of all I love Vermont because of her indomitable people." Now, those emotionally charged words are history. His words were nuggets of gold for many Vermonters including my father.

My father was a sixth generation Vermonter. He wanted his children to love Vermont as much as he did. His words and actions fostered in us a love for our surroundings. And so, my siblings and I loved the surrounding rolling hills of our farm covering about two hundred acres nestled among the green hills and valleys of Central Vermont. Our home and the surrounding cattle barn, milk house, and old horse barn sat on the crest of a hill. From our home, we saw our maple orchard and woodlot in one direction. Our pastures and hay meadows to the west and south and our cultivated land of many vegetable crops to the north and east cast beautiful panoramic views. Our nearest neighbors were almost a mile away.

In addition to my three sisters, my family consisted of my mother and father and three older brothers. In 1954, my father was fifty-five years old; my mother was forty-three. Gene was nineteen and had been in the United States Army for two years, having left home as soon as he graduated from high school. Clarence was next at eighteen and Raymond was fifteen. We sisters followed.

It is said that everyone has a story to tell. Here is an opportunity to travel back with me to the fifties, and experience my life growing up in rural Vermont. Learn about the work involved in operating and living on a dairy farm. Come with me and read about my family. You'll learn about many of my family experiences as we tackled jobs that needed to be done on our farm. And none of us except Dad owned a Social Security card!

Chapter 1

PREPARING AND PLANTING OUR CASH CROPS

When tillage begins, the arts follow. The farmers, therefore,
are the founders of human civilization.
Daniel Webster

In addition to our dairy cows and maple sugaring operation, my father had other money-making ventures on our farm. Among those were cash crops of corn, potatoes, and several varieties of squash. Clarence and Dad were involved in the many steps of planting crops usually beginning in late May after the last frost of the spring season.

As soon as the maple sugaring season ended, my dad began to think about and prepare for the summer season.

"The sap buckets, lids, and spouts are washed, dried, and stored until another season rolls around. Now I can tend to other things that need to be done around here," he said as I helped him put away the old washtub.

He tended to such matters as seed and fertilizer purchases. His checklist included corn seeds, seeds for the four varieties of squash, and every kind of seed needed for our vegetable garden. He whistled softly to himself as he worked his way through the seed catalog. A new project was in the making and Dad ordered oat seeds.

"There, all the seeds are ordered. They'll be here soon. I'm glad for summer, aren't you, Pat? Look how green the grass is and do you see how the maple leaves have suddenly popped out of their buds? Those cold winters have been felt all the way to my aching bones. I'm glad for summer," he repeated as he ruffled up my hair.

"Me, too. I like it when everything turns green and I like the flowers, too," I replied.

Next, Dad checked all the fences to be certain there were no weak links between the cedar posts.

"Mrs. Farnsworth will let us know if the cows break through the fencing and get into her garden," Dad chuckled. "No cow or heifer will get through the fence this year. I've repaired every weak link."

Clarence eliminated any worry about getting the plowing and preparation of the soil ready for the planting season. He, too, was happy for warmer weather and went about his work with a quicker step.

"The fields are ready for the corn and the potatoes," Clarence said after plowing, harrowing, and fertilizing each one with our machinery.

Next, Dad's attention was given to tubers. Tubers grow underground. From a planted tuber a new plant will develop. The new growing tuber must stay in the soil until it is harvested. If it is exposed to the sun, it

A Farmall tractor similar to the one used on our farm.

turns greenish-yellow and loses its flavor and nutrients. Of course woodchucks favored these exposed tubers as a snack.

"Our potatoes will disappear if they grow above ground," Dad said. "The woodchucks will gnaw at every one."

I sat right beside Dad on the porch in the warm sun and helped him prepare the potatoes. Lots of people in Vermont were happy to feel the warm sun on their face and arms after a long cold winter and we were no different.

"Pat, if you're going to help, be careful with that knife and every potato piece must have an eye or two in it," he said.

"An eye? What's an eye? What do you mean?" I asked

sheepishly for I thought my dad was kidding.

"Every tuber has several eyes, something like buds. From the eyes, roots will develop underground. Leaves and stems will develop above ground. So when you cut, be careful. Watch me."

I watched as Dad rapidly cut a large potato into four or five pieces. Dad's hands were very large. He held two or three potatoes in one hand as he cut each into a few pieces.

"See?" he said. I noticed the little depression, an eye in each piece.

The potatoes fell plunk, plunk, plunk into the pail of water at his feet so that the eyes could have a head start in the warming soil. He filled pail after pail with potatoes.

The potato itself provided nourishment for the new plant as it began to grow. Most of the time, we used our own potatoes. Other times we purchased potatoes for planting to increase productivity using a different variety. Dad favored a variety called Green Mountain potatoes.

"They're the best," he had said many times. "Nice white Green Mountain potatoes."

"That's the right way, Pat," Dad said as he encouraged me. "One eye to a customer! At least one to each tuber!"

I had to be careful to remember an eye for each piece

and to watch out for my fingers. No cut fingers needed! No potatoes without an eye either!

You can see what a long and tedious job it must have been to prepare the seed potatoes for planting. Even with all the work that needed to be done, Dad was happiest at this time of year. He whistled while he worked and enjoyed the warm, just-right sunny days. I knew Dad was older than most of my friends' dads and he often spoke about his "aching bones" especially in the winter.

Because our farm had so many potatoes to plant, Dad owned a special planter pulled by the tractor that automatically sowed the potatoes. My brother Clarence filled the planter with the cut potatoes and hauled it to the field. You could follow his trail because water dribbled out as he drove along across the driveway and down the road to the ready-to-plant field.

When he reached the field, Clarence dropped a special lever on the planter to allow the potato pieces to roll out onto the ground one or two at a time. One part of the planter dug narrow rows in the dirt. Then a little plow-like piece of the planter covered every potato with soil three or four inches deep. That was deep enough to keep woodchucks, mice, and other animals from finding them. Clarence moved along the field on the tractor and planted six rows at a time.

Every once in a while he checked to see if there were

still potatoes in the planter. When the planter was empty, Clarence returned to the house and refilled the machine with more potatoes.

"It's warm enough today for the plants to root right
away." Clarence removed his cap and wiped sweat from
his forehead with his handkerchief.

"You're right about that!" replied Dad. He helped Clarence refill the planter. "Summer is early this year. It is
so warm, there's no danger of frost."

By the end of May, all of the potatoes had been planted, all seven acres. Soon the eyes in the potatoes began their work just as Clarence and Dad had predicted.
Little green shoots shot up from under the ground as if
by magic. At the same time, roots were developing deep
within the soil.

The corn was planted using the same machinery. Our
machine expert, Clarence, had figured out how to allow
the small corn kernels to fall through the planter slowly
just as the potatoes had. By rigging up some metal to
make the holes smaller for the corn kernels, the planter
deposited six rows of corn seeds at a time.

By the time I was eleven my father had modernized
our farm with tractors and plenty of machinery. The
farm horses had been put out to pasture and long ago
had left our farm.

"Our tractor and machines are busier than we are.
They do all the work while we watch," Dad joked.

Corn fields

Dad planted the squash without any special equipment. All he needed was a hoe. After the soil had been
tilled, just as in the corn and potato fields, he used the
hoe to create hill-like mounds. There in the mounds,
he planted the squash seeds: the big blue Hubbards,
the green buttercups and acorns, and the tan colored
butternuts. Soon, little green seedlings would peep up
through the soil warmed by the sun and moistened by
recent showers.

Raymond planted a couple of his scarecrows, one in
the center of the potato field and one in the squash field.
The scarecrows were created using two slender pieces
of wood nailed together like a T. They contained dented
old, but still shiny pie pans, old hats and mittens, and

Squash plants

colorful ribbons and yarns.

"My scarecrows will keep away the nasty crows be-cause they look like you little kids," Raymond kidded.

"Oh, Raymee, you say the nicest things! Doesn't he, Patty?" Sandy replied.

"You'll get a pat on the back from Raymee," I agreed with a laugh.

At dinnertime on that planting day, Clarence said, "If the weather stays as warm as it is today, the corn will be knee high by the Fourth of July."

"The tubers are in the ground. It's all up to nature now," declared my satisfied dad. "Let's hope nature is good to us this season. The weather so far has been perfect. That job is done. Now we can move on to other tasks. Let's hope Raymond's scarecrows keep all the critters away including the deer."

Within a short time, our fields quickly changed from the color of earth to ever-growing shades of green. And, Dad kept his eye on the weather. Too hard a rain could cause a washout!

Chapter 2

PLANTING AND WORKING IN THE GARDEN

*One hears a lot about the rules of good husbandry; there is only one–
leave the land far better than you found it.*
George Henderson

My family seldom purchased vegetables or fruits from the grocery store. We rarely bought meat, bread, cakes or pies. Were we hungry? Do you think we disliked fresh vegetables and fruits? Did we long for fresh appetizing treats? Not on your life! We enjoyed veggies, fruits, and meats without shopping at a grocery store.

We raised animals. My dad sold most of the little piglets, but we always kept one for ourselves. We kept a male calf instead of selling it for veal to the cattle dealer. When the calf was full grown, as with the pig, we slaughtered it for food.

Mom baked our bread. Ray, Harriet, and Carolyn often were busy in the kitchen making pies, cakes, and other goodies.

We used many fruits that grew around our farm. A huge crabapple tree produced fruit for crabapple jelly. Our old apple orchard provided fruit to eat fresh, or to make baked apples, cider, applesauce, cakes, muffins and pies. We harvested wild grapes for grape juice and jellies. We picked tiny chokeberries and after our mom processed them with lots of sugar, we enjoyed another kind of jelly. From our raspberry patch, during July we picked juicy berries for jams and pies. My family gathered tiny wild, red strawberries that peeked up through the green grasses that grew along the fields and roadsides in late May and early June. Wild blackberries were collected for pies and jams in August. A rhubarb patch provided the main ingredient for rhubarb pies and rhubarb sauce to pour over ice cream.

Once a year, we piled into our car to ride to a neighbor's cherry orchard to pick cherries for cobblers and pies. We spent one Sunday every August traveling to Enfield, New Hampshire, to pick teeny tiny blueberries.

Our garden was plentiful with all kinds of vegetables, everything from A to Z. During May and early June my siblings and I planted vegetables.

Mom processed food for our use in the winter. She canned and froze many of our garden vegetables. Canned goods were stored in our basement. Now you know why we were not hungry because most of our food came from our land or surrounding area and from our animals.

In late May, with the snow gone until another winter, my brother Clarence said, "Our cash crops are planted.

Now it's time to spread manure on the garden plot. We'll plant the garden."

Clarence used our tractor and plow to turn the soil, to break up the sod, and to mix the manure into the soil. And finally he pulled the harrow over the plowed area. The sharp disks on the harrow were circular in shape as a pie, and were forced into the soil by the heavy rocks that sat on top of the machine. This machine smoothed and broke up the heavy clumps of dirt and further mixed the manure with the soil. Some harrows, called cultivators, had sharp, heavy steel objects that looked like pointed teeth.

The teeth broke up and smoothed the soil just as the disks did. Whether a farmer had a harrow with disks or a cultivator with teeth, each machine accomplished the same job. When Clarence finished his work, the soil looked smooth, but an occasional rock peeped up through the soil.

Sometimes we added extra fertilizer using another special machine. Always the guy at the tractor's wheel, Clarence spread a thin layer of the grayish white fertilizer over the garden.

With the tilling of the soil complete, Clarence declared, "Girls, it's your turn. You can take over."

"Yes, Clarence, that smelly cow manure will help our garden grow!" laughed Sandy. Clarence grinned.

Carolyn added, "That's our 'Evening in Paris.' "

"Yes," I said to myself, "this is the time of year when our land seeps with the odor of earth and barn manure."

A few days earlier, Dad had said, "Pat, get one of the old pails and soak the peas in water. They'll sprout and grow more quickly. Each pea will have a head start."

Now Dad emptied the pail of its water to expose the sprouting peas. "Here you are, Pat. Take these to the garden."

"Okay!" My pace was slowed by the heavy weight of the pail and its contents.

Earlier, my sisters and I kept an eye on the tomato and cabbage seeds that we had planted in moistened dirt-filled wooden boxes. Nearly every day we watered the seedlings as they began to grow. The boxes had been set by the kitchen windows and soaked up each morning's sun. Little green tomato and light green cabbage seedlings soon sprouted. Like the peas, they were ready to plant. Harriet, Carolyn, Sandy, and I carried the heavy boxes to the garden.

Our hand rakes, hoes, spades, and other tools no longer sat idle on their hooks in the woodshed. Hand rakes smoothed out any small sod chunks left by Clarence's harrow.

Carolyn directed Sandy to get the old wheelbarrow to collect the rocks.

"That's the worst job. I don't want to do that!" said

Sandy impulsively.

Carolyn said nothing and eventually Sandy wheeled the Randolph wheelbarrow over to the garden. Stones that had decided to surface over the long winter were collected and Carolyn and Sandy wheeled the rocks over to our ever-growing rock pile.

Sandy mimicked Dad, "I'd like a nickel for every rock I've carried off this garden!"

"Hop in!" Carolyn said as she pushed the wheelbarrow around the grassy edge of the garden.

Sandy enjoyed a thirty-second ride laughing and taunting Carolyn. "Faster, Carolyn! Can't you go any faster?"

"Be nice or I'll tip you over into this wonderful smelling dirt. You're getting too heavy for this wheelbarrow."

"You go to the end of the garden, Pat, and push this stick into the dirt," Harriet instructed as she tied string to the stick and handed it to me. "Never mind the clowns."

"Okay, Harriet," and even though my eyes were on Sandy's wheelbarrow ride, I hurried to the garden's end and forced the stick into the soil.

"I'll cut the twine on my end after I tie my stick to it and it will make nice straight rows. We'll use this twine as a guide for every row of vegetables," Harriet continued.

We planted row after row of peas and other vegetables

this way.

Harriet had a plan. "I'll take the spade and make little holes in the ground. You little kids put one tomato plant into each hole. Then I'll dig more holes for the cabbages."

Carolyn grabbed the hoe. "I'll tamp the dirt down all around the plants to hold them in place." Soon the wooden boxes were empty.

"You little kids clean the boxes with the watering hose and put them away," ordered Harriet.

Sandy and I, box in hand, went back and forth until every one was rinsed and was safely stored in the shed.

"That task is finished, now we can move on to other things." I repeated my father's words.

Carolyn got a hammer from Clarence's toolbox, "I'll pound these wooden stakes into the ground near the tomatoes. In a week or so, we'll tie the tomato stems to the stakes. They'll grow straight and tall."

We knew that the fruit would not be crowded and each heavy plant had a ready-made anchor, the stick and twine. The tomatoes were healthier because they would not grow mold by touching or falling into the damp soil. Carefully, we girls opened the seed packets, one by one, and planted long rows of the other vegetables: carrots, spinach, Swiss chard, turnips, beets, parsnips, lettuce, radishes, onion bulbs, cucumbers, and summer

Tomato plants

squash.

"Hey, you and Sandy save the seed packets. Put them over the tops of the little sticks at the beginning of each row," Harriet reminded us.

"Why?" Sandy asked. "The rain will only ruin them."

"Sandy, you little kids know why. We need to know which plants are which. By the time the packets wear out, the vegetables will be growing."

Harriet dug a little trench with a hoe the full length of each row, using the string and stick. "Look how nice and straight these rows are."

"I'll sprinkle the seeds," offered Carolyn. "And Sandy, use the hoe to cover the seeds with dirt."

"Okay. I'll use the other hoe to tamp down the dirt covering the seeds," I said. "That will keep the chipmunks and squirrels from digging for them."

We switched tasks, taking turns completing various parts of the planting. We worked with good humor, enjoying the sunny day, each of us trading off one job for another. The day passed quickly.

"I'm going into sixth grade, Sandy. Mrs. Abbot already told me that I'm passing with flying colors," I bragged. "I think you'll pass, too. You've done all of your work, haven't you, Sandy?"

"Yeah, well, most of it. Why did she tell you that you're passing and not me? I hope I pass."

"I dunno, but she said that if I read this summer, I can get a head start on sixth grade. That's really all she said."

"I hope I pass," Sandy repeated. "I did most of my work."

It was time to change the subject. "Let's get the straw, Sandy. We'll spread it all around."

"Okay, Patty."

We struggled with the heavy straw bales that had been placed around our house's foundation for the winter. Like a blanket, it had kept our vegetables stored in the basement from freezing. Now the straw had a new use.

Harriet used a sharp knife to open each bale of straw by cutting the twine that held it together. With our hands, Carolyn, Sandy, and I fluffed up it up and spread it among the rows. That kept the weeds from growing.

Sandy and I threw the straw here and there shouting, "Look! It's raining straw! Head for cover!"

"Let's get this work finished. You two little kids tend to business. I don't want to be out here all day," Harriet reminded us.

"We're making hay while the sun shines," Sandy said, laughing.

Overall, we sisters were good at working together. Working in the garden was a favorite job. We were no longer in need of winter coats, and the sun felt wonderful as it warmed our faces, arms, and hearts.

"It's important to work together to get things accomplished," our dad would say. And all of us did just that with the exception of Raymond who was most likely working in the family kitchen baking pies, cakes, breads or other goodies for our large family. He was Mother's main helper. He suffered from wheezing, coughing, and allergies.

Dad showed us how to do many things around the farm. Making good use of our time was important to him and he often judged others by what they accomplished with their time.

"Whoever made time, made a lot of it," he proclaimed. "So let's make good use of it. Let's not waste it. And remember, many hands make light work."

Sandy often asked with a smile, "Daddy, if you add

another number to the clock, will we have more time?"

Dad often responded to Sandy's fun by not saying a word. Instead, with a hearty laugh, he playfully messed up her blond hair with one big hand. As for me, I never tired of Sandy's questions.

We planted many different types of beans including pole beans, bush beans, soldier beans, string beans, wax beans, great northern beans, all kinds of beans. The pole beans were planted in little mounds or hills in a circular fashion.

When the pole beans started to grow, Sandy and I helped Dad place cedar posts seven or eight feet in length into the center of each of the bean hills.

"Darn, Pat, I forgot to bring the posthole digger from the barn. Can you little kids run to the barn and get it? I'll get the hammer and the sledgehammer from the shed."

"All right," I said. "Let's run, Sandy! I can win!"

"You don't have a chance, Patty." Indeed, Sandy quickly outdistanced me. I felt destined to be the shortest of everybody at times like that. "Just once I'd like to run faster," I said to myself.

"Hold the cedar posts nice and straight, Sandy." Dad had dug deep holes with the posthole digger. He used the heavy sledgehammer and forced the cedar posts, one at a time, into the holes.

I gathered up another post and passed it to Dad as he

built the trellis for the beanstalks.

"Okay, now you little kids tamp down the soil nice and tight all around the posts."

Next, Sandy and I wove several layers of twine that connected the posts together. Dad used u-shaped nails and with the hammer nailed the twine to the posts. The finished twine looked like a musical staff.

"There that's done, now the young beans have something to hold on to as they grow," Dad chimed in. "Now we can move on to other things that need to be done around here."

As the beans grew, Sandy observed, "Look at them! They're growing just like Jack and the Giant Beanstalk!"

With the help of the manure, the fertilizer, a warm sun, and soil moistened by rain, our plants grew into beautiful rows of vegetables. Soon weeds poked their way up through the layer of straw. We pulled them out. Pesky weeds will selfishly take over a garden if given a good start. Crabgrass, kale, dandelions, thistles, misplaced daisies, milkweed seedlings, and others were pulled up by their roots to make way for a weed-free garden.

You can see why, with all this garden produce, we rarely bought vegetables at the grocery store. Special holidays required a trip to the store, perhaps for yams or sweet potatoes and cranberries for a Thanksgiving Day feast. Or a watermelon on the Fourth of July! We

Vegetables growing in straight rows

enjoyed fresh oranges from Florida at Christmas.

"Bananas come to us all the way from the tropics," Dad boasted when Mom bought them at a reduced price. "Mom will make banana bread and banana cream pies with those that are about to go."

"Raymee makes banana muffins with some of those old bananas," Sandy added.

"We have everything we need from our garden except salt for the salt shaker." My self-reliant dad beamed with happiness over our produce. "There is nothing better than fresh vegetables on the table."

We kids knew how lucky we were ever since those poor kids had moved into the old house down the road from us. They didn't have enough to eat and they never had gone to a dentist. Their teeth were black and their eyes were way deep in their faces.

Sandy said, "At school, nobody talks to them at recess. They're afraid of them and I am, too."

Everyone shied away from the kids, even Bobby. They didn't have any socks and their shoes were full of holes. They had no laces.

Mom appreciated our dad. "He's the salt of the earth. God threw away the mold when he was created."

Sometimes I'd mimic Dad after we completed chores. "That task is finished. Now we can move on to something else. And we have one less thing to worry about." Dad would always laugh when he heard me.

Chapter 3

WRESTLING WITH WEEDS

A weed is no more than a flower in disguise.
James Russell Lowell

"You think this kale is so pretty? Well, just wait until you've pulled a row or two and then tell us how pretty everything is, Patty!" Raymond said as we began wrestling with the weeds.

I stopped my weeding, looked at the tall kale that I had just pulled, its sun-yellow blossoms, its long stem, and roots. "The kale IS pretty. The potatoes' green leaves and yellow kale blossoms look beautiful together."

"I suppose you think the other weeds are beautiful, too? Oh, lookee here, what a beautiful ragweed!"

More important than the garden weeding, more important than almost any activity that required our labor, was the use of our hands. "Many hands make light work," Dad always said.

I worked my way up one row and down another with Raymond and my sisters. I wore my cotton gloves. Though my hands were hot and sweaty, I remembered Dad's words. "You know what Dr. Woodruff told you about your allergies, Pat. You need those gloves."

"Okay, Dad." I made sure my gloves were in my pocket

Kale needs pulling!

whenever we were getting ready to work.

Raymond, the youngest of my three brothers, often said, "I hate this job!" But he, my sisters, and I kept right on pulling the weeds.

"My hands are too hot for gloves! How can you stand to wear them? It's so hot! It's way too hot! I can't breathe!" Raymond complained.

Ragweed was the culprit this time. Raymond suffered from allergies and coughed, sneezed, and wheezed and sounded as if he suffered from a nasty cold.

"Okay," Raymond said after a few more minutes of weed pulling. "It's time for our break. Let's have a drink of Kool-Aid. Where's the thermos?"

"I'll get it. It's over in the shade where our dog is

sprawled out. She's hot, too, that wonderful collie," Sandy said.

We followed Sandy as she ran to the shady oasis. "I get to drink first because I got here first." Sandy uncapped the thermos and began a long cold drink.

"Come on, little kid, that's enough," Raymond groaned.

"What do you say? What's the password, Raymee?"

"Gimme the thermos!"

Sandy handed it over and Raymond enjoyed a long cool drink, and sat down in the grass. "Here you are, Carolyn."

"Thanks." Carolyn held the thermos, took a cool drink, smacked her lips, too. "Here Harriet, it's icy cold, a cherry flavor."

Harriet drank and the red liquid dribbled down her chin and onto her shirt. "Oh, that's sweet! Did you mix it, Ray?"

"Hey! Save some for me. My throat is dry and I am so thirsty!" I whined.

"Don't worry, Patty! There's a lot in there," said Sandy.

Harriet passed the thermos to me. "Here, Pat, have a drink."

How good it felt as the coolness slipped all the way down to my tummy. I guzzled and swallowed, guzzled and swallowed. "Cherry's my favorite." I was breathless as I passed the thermos on to Sandy.

"Raymee, did you mix the Kool-Aid?" Sandy asked.

"You betcha, kid! I put in an extra scoop of sugar just for you."

We soon returned to work. "Ouch! The grassy weeds just cut my fingers!" I screamed. No one spoke. I quickly pulled my gloves from my pocket and put them on. "My fingers are burning, Harriet. Harriet, my fingers are cut!"

"Put your gloves on and forget about it," Harriet said.

As I worked, I paused to look at the roots, something I had done before. "Sandy, take a look at these roots. There is one long, long one. And there are little roots growing all over the place like little ropes. No wonder they are so hard to pull up."

"Yeah, that's why I'm only pulling the tops of the weeds."

"If you do that, the weeds grow right back."

"Okay, Patty, I'll try to get the roots, too." Sandy frowned and picked up a daisy.

Our task became tiresome after a couple of days of pulling the tall kale, the stringy grasses with tough-to-pull roots, pesky ragweed, the bright yellow buttercups, the dandelions, and other weeds. Sandy and I had stopped our weed pulling many times to play a favorite game.

Sandy removed one white daisy petal at a time saying, "He loves me. He loves me not. He loves me!" And when the last petal was removed, she joyfully exclaimed, "Oh, my! He loves me!"

"Who loves you?" I asked.

"I'm not telling. That's for me to know and for you to find out."

"I bet it's Johnny because he picked you for his team at school."

Sandy smiled. "And, when you win with a 'he loves me,' I suppose that's Bobby?" Sandy laughed and tossed the daisy up in the air.

"Maybe," I answered.

As soon as we finished the weeding, my father checked the leafy green potato plants to see if blight or other fungus was developing on the young plants. If he determined that, yes, they had fungus, he or Clarence got out the sprayer and mixed fungicide with water and sprayed it on the potato plants using the tractor. The fungicide ended any spread of the dreaded blight disease.

Potato blight or tip burn can be caused by drought, a lack of water. The tips of the leaves turn brown and eventually wrinkle the leaf. Left unattended, the whole plant can die. Too much water can cause blight, too. Insect attacks may be another cause of blight. Cutworms can attack the young plant and cause spotty discoloration or a moldy looking leaf. That can cause a plant to die if unattended.

I was with Dad on the day he inspected his potatoes.

Potato blossoms

"We're in luck this year, Pat. There's no sign of the enemy."

"That's one less thing to worry about, Dad." I looked up to see Dad smiling at me.

Dad grew the potato variety called Green Mountain potatoes. "They're the best," he repeated often. "I've tried other varieties. In Maine, farmers like the Kennebec variety. I've tried those. I've tried the Yukon Gold type. However, Green Mountains are the best. With our four varieties of squash and the tender sweet corn, we have good cash crops. They're our bread and butter."

"It's the cows that give us butter and Mom who gives us bread baked with the flour she buys at the A & P," Sandy stated. Dad laughed and playfully messed up

Sandy's hair.

We felt lucky to be able to grow so much of our own food. Keeping the fields free of weeds was a daunting but necessary task.

At supper after a long weed-pulling day, Mom said, "Today, Mrs. Boyden called. The cherries are ready."

"Yippee!" Sandy and I exclaimed.

"We can pick the cherries as soon as the fields are weeded," Mom added.

Dad spoke up, "You children have tackled the fields. Go get the cherries with your mother in the morning. Don't go horsing around on the ladders. Be careful."

"Raymee, will you bake us a cherry cobbler?" Sandy asked.

Chapter 4

HARVESTING CHERRIES

I cannot tell a lie, I cut the cherry tree with my hatchet.
Attributed to George Washington

Harriet and Carolyn returned to the kitchen and both said at once, "All of the pails are in the car. Let's go!"

"The front seat is for me!" Raymond grabbed the thermos jug filled with Kool-Aid and headed for the car.

Nearly in unison, Carolyn and Harriet said, "I have a window seat," and that, of course, meant that Sandy and I sat crammed in between them like the lettuce and tomato in a sandwich.

It was a special day early in the summer after the planting and in the middle of the weeding that we headed to Boyden's cherry orchard. Mom drove the old, blue Plymouth sedan.

"Why can't I drive?" asked Raymond. "I'm old enough."

"You know as well as I that as soon as you have your license you'll be able to drive with the girls in the car. Until then, Dad forbids you to drive with anyone except me," Mom answered calmly.

"I'm a safe driver, and I don't go too fast," argued Ray. Mom said nothing more about it.

The car's trunk carried anything that had handles: old, leaky milk pails, rusted sap bucket pails, dented lard pails and much-used peanut butter cans. Just name it, if it had a handle, it was useful for holding cherries. Old stuff was never thrown out because Dad's motto was "Use it up. Wear it out. Make it do. Or do without." Too often Dad said those old words.

"Raymee, will you bake me some cherry cobbler? You know how I like it so!" Sandy begged.

"Yes, but only if you and the other little kid don't embarrass me in front of anybody."

"Oh, Raymond, leave the little kids alone," Harriet responded. "Don't you ever tire of picking on them?" Raymond laughed.

At the orchard we eagerly climbed out of the cramped car, opened the trunk, and Harriet handed each of us an old pail. Raymond set the large ones beside the car.

"Hi there." Mr. Boyden wore a big grin when he met us at the edge of his orchard. "Come this way." We followed him.

"Edna's got coffee ready," he nodded to my mother who then turned and walked down the lane to visit with Mrs. Boyden. Mom was always happy when she had the opportunity to visit with her friends.

"Ladders are all around here. Grab one and lean it against the tree and you'll be able to reach the highest cherries. Most folks who come here don't like to use the ladders." Mr. Boyden pointed to the ladders.

And so each of us carried or dragged a ladder, leaned

it against a tree trunk, climbed it while we carried a pail, and steadied ourselves with one free hand. Once up the ladder and with one outstretched arm, we gathered the small red cherries one by one.

"What a rickety old ladder! I hope I don't crash to earth," Sandy complained.

"Be careful not to fall," I cautioned.

"Well if I do fall, it isn't very far."

"Falling off the couch wasn't very far either but you broke your collar bone. Remember?"

"My pail is full," I heard Carolyn, and then Harriet, and then Raymond say. Sandy and I glanced at each other as we struggled to fill our pails.

"Mine is full," I said after a few more minutes.

"Mine too," said Sandy and she and I each clambered down a wobbly ladder and poured the cherries into our bigger buckets. Time after time ...

"Finally, we've filled these old pails. Egad!" Raymond tried to lift one. "These are heavy!"

Mr. Boyden, who had also been harvesting for other customers, said, "Let me help you load these pails into your car, young man."

"They have to go in the trunk. We kids take up all the seat spaces," Sandy explained.

"Yeah, right. You Chase kids sure have picked a lot of cherries. Edna says that you all know how to get things done." Mr. Boyden looked closely at the produce and figured out how much we had picked.

"Yes, all the work I have been doing since I was knee high to a grasshopper got me a job with the Bigelows at their lodge in Randolph." Raymond laughed at his own joke.

"Oh, what do you do there? Aren't you still in school?"

"Of course I'm still in high school! I'm almost a sophomore! I work after school and on weekends when Mrs. Bigleow needs a baker or a waiter or someone to run errands for her."

Mr. Boyden nodded and with pencil and paper headed for his house. We kids waited outside while Mom paid him.

"Thank you for the coffee. Good-bye, Edna," Mom called as she left their house.

"Nice to see you today, Mary. It sure is a nice day for being outside. Come and see me again soon."

Mom nodded and headed for the car. "I'd like that. See you soon."

At home, we carried the cherries into our kitchen.

"Help me with this, one of you," Mom said. "Pour cold water into the dishpan."

"All right," volunteered Carolyn.

Mom and Carolyn began the long process of rinsing the cherries. Harriet got out our biggest pots. "I'll fill these pots with water to steam the cherries."

"Rinse them first, Harriet. They've been sitting in the

Pails much like these were used for cherry picking

storeroom for a long time."

Within minutes, Mom and Carolyn dumped the cherries into the pots, gallon after gallon. "Oh, they smell so good!" exclaimed Sandy when the cherries became steamy.

Raymond was helpful. "I'll get our lunch." He opened the refrigerator and removed the bowl of coleslaw and the platter of egg salad sandwiches that he had prepared for a quick lunch.

"Soup's on!" he announced with a laugh.

Harriet opened the fridge. "Who wants some milk?"

"I do! And Patty wants some, too," Sandy answered.

After lunch the fun began! The cherries had cooled, and now we removed the pits and stems from each cherry. I knew how to pick and how to pit. I was careful not to miss a one.

"These cherry pits are as hard as stones," Sandy said.

"They're dangerous if bitten into while enjoying a piece of pie. That's what Daddy says," I added.

"Dentists have enough to do without mending a cracked or broken tooth," Dad had warned us.

"Imagine if your teeth were as sharp as tacks because the edges had broken off. How would you keep from stabbing your tongue?" Sandy's quips made us laugh.

I told Sandy, "Your mind is as sharp as a tack. Your brain is surviving quite well. But, I'm worried about your tongue."

She and I loved to joke around and we giggled at each other's jokes. We stuck together.

With every pit removed, Carolyn asked, "Mom how much sugar do I add to the cherries?"

Mom dumped a lot of sugar into the huge pot. "That looks like enough. Stir it well."

After this job was done, Sandy and I completed a good deed with the pits outside. "One, two, three," Sandy and I counted and then spat the pit as far as we could. We never grew tired of this diversion from our busy day nor did we keep score of who spit farther.

Raymond, often exasperated with us, scolded, "You little kids think of the craziest things! What will you do next?"

"Oh, Raymond leave the little kids alone. You're old enough to know that they need to let off steam! They're

A beaver's teeth cut this tree.

not harming anyone." Dad grew weary of Ray's teasing.

Our game with the cherry pits kept our little animal friends happy. Sandy and I scattered the remaining cherry pits near our raspberry patch so that birds, squirrels, chipmunks, and other animals could have something new to eat.

The birds had no teeth to worry about. But chipmunks and squirrels have ever-growing teeth. They didn't have to worry about breaking or chipping a tooth. The more any rodent uses its teeth for cutting and chewing, the faster they grow. Beavers have a reputation for being busy so they keep their teeth in check.

While we were pitting the cherries, Raymond got busy making cherry pies. He began by mixing a great batch of pie-crust dough, enough to create two pies at a time.

After he mixed the crusts' ingredients of flour, lard, salt, and water, he divided the dough into four equal portions. He kneaded the dough after sprinkling it with flour. He rolled it out, one part at a time, into a flat circular shape with the rolling pin. Then, he carefully folded the dough in half and lifted the dough into the pie pan.

Next, he arranged the dough to fit the pan perfectly like a glove to your hand, and trimmed away the rough edges with the crimper. He added the sweetened cherry mixture. Soon the top crust was in its place and attached around the edges of the pan to the bottom crust. Raymond continued until both pies were ready for the oven.

"I'm making something special today. I'm going to make everyone an individual pie. I'll make more dough. When the dough is ready, I'll roll out a little bit at a time to make a little circle," Raymond murmured to himself. "And, now here goes some sweet cherries on one side of my circle."

Sandy and I watched as he continued. He folded one half of the crust gently over the other half to form a crescent shape, something like a half moon. He created pretty designs along the edge of the crust using a fork. Occasionally, he created a special tart for each of us.

"Here's an S for Sandy and here's a P for Pat, the little kids," he'd tell himself as he worked.

As the cherry tarts baked in the electric oven, the hot sugary contents bubbled up onto the top crust.

"I can smell your tarts! I smell your pies! Can we have dessert first?" asked Sandy as Raymond removed the bubbling treats from the oven. "They look scrumptious!"

"No, you need a square meal first."

With the remaining fruit, Raymond baked cherry cobbler, one of Sandy's favorites. A cobbler is baked in a deep dish similar to a cake pan. One or two cake-like crusts were used. When served warm, a dollop of ice cream, Hood of course, plunked on top became warm and trickled down and all around the cobbler.

"This is Raymond's best dessert." Sandy smacked her lips and reached for a second serving at supper.

"I made it just for you, kid."

"Thank you, Raymee! Oh, thank you!"

The cherries that were not immediately used were stored and frozen in quart-sized containers for use during the winter. Each container had just enough sugar and cherries for one pie.

"Carolyn, use the special pen and write on each container," Mom said.

"Yes. I'll write 'Sweetened Cherries, 1954.' " She rapidly began to write.

"Carolyn has excellent cursive writing skills," Miss Flanders had commented on her report card. Miss Flanders, like all Carolyn's other teachers, was proud of my sister's cooperation and work ethic at school.

Sandy and I carried the packaged cherries to the freezer. Harriet stacked all the packages next to the few frozen fruits left over from last season's harvest. Harriet made sure each package was placed so that the contents were easy to identify when needed during the long winter. We were a team with a mission. Teamwork was our specialty.

Our freezer was located in a special room behind the kitchen. It contained three compartments, each sporting a lid with a knob. When any compartment was opened, there before you was Harriet's handiwork.

"The first compartment is for vegetables, the middle has fruits, and the third has all of our meat," Harriet explained.

Raymond baked many kinds of pies. Along with his cherry pies, he baked rhubarb, apple, pumpkin, squash, raspberry, and blueberry pies. You name it! He was a fine baker. We loved him for that.

During the month of George Washington's birthday, Raymond thawed frozen cherries.

"Happy Birthday, George," he'd say, as he carved a cherry with a little stem on the top crust. "Now, don't go chopping down any more cherry trees! Because of you, February is a special time to enjoy cherry delights."

Soon Harriet and Carolyn were making pies and they were just as delicious as Raymond's. Harriet created a better piecrust by adding sugar and a little butter to the bottom crust before she added the pie mixture. She called that her "secret ingredient." She was the expert at baking apple pies.

"I'm going to find your recipe one of these days," warned Raymond.

"Never!" Harriet said.

"All good things must come to an end," Sandy often said after enjoying a tasty dessert.

Dad chuckled at Sandy's remarks, and with one hand scuffed up her hair. With a twinkle in his eye, he winked and nodded in appreciation of her humor. Sandy was the apple of Dad's eye. We loved our dad for we were all the apple of his eye in one way or another.

At suppertime that day, Mom said, "We were all so taken up by the cherries that I finally had a chance to go through the mail while you were calling in the cows. Gene will be home next week. His letter came while we were at Boyden's orchard. He's leaving San Francisco to-morrow."

"Gene! Gene's coming home! When will he be here?" I asked.

"He bought a car and a buddy is helping him drive as far as Cleveland. He wants to be here in five days," Mom answered.

I couldn't wait to see Gene again.

"Look at Sandy," Clarence chuckled. "She's dancing around the table!"

Chapter 5

A SLICE OF PIE

*Happy families are all alike; every unhappy family
is unhappy in its own way.*
Anna Karenina

"Pat, you've got to understand some things. There is nothing you or I can do to change everything to the way we'd like it. Get over your sadness about Gene. He has made up his mind about what he's going to do with his life. Life goes on," Dad said when he knew I was down in the dumps over Gene's decision.

Dad was right; I was dragging my feet and full of gloom, doom, and despair. Summer vacation had begun and Sandy asked me all the time, "Come on Pat, Let's get on our bikes. Let's go for a ride." Or, "Let's go down to the brook."

"Don't feel like it," I'd mumble. "It's too hot."

But I continued daily chores with the rest of us kids. We four sisters soon began our next venture on the farm. Our brother Raymond waited in the kitchen for our produce, his allergies preventing him from venturing out with us. In early summer, our rhubarb patch came to life. When rhubarb is planted, it grows by itself every year and the patch will take root, spread, and choke anything growing nearby. It is as predictable as grass growing after a long winter or the dandelions popping up every spring. It has been used as food for centuries.

"Pat, you don't want to end up with any missing fingers. Be careful with that knife. Sandra, leave the job to your older sisters," Dad said.

Sandy always replied, "Okay, Daddy. I'll leave it all to the big kids. I'll take a ride on my bike."

"Oh, Sandy, you have to help, too. You can help me," I'd pipe up.

Sometimes I was caught in the middle between being a big kid and a little kid. I thought it was okay to be more grown up but that left Sandy as the only little one. I didn't want her to feel left out.

So, my sisters and I made our way to the ever-expanding rhubarb patch just east of the barn.

"This rhubarb patch is taking up more space every year," Carolyn noted. "It's a good thing it's here in the pasture and not in our garden. Look at how it has spread all around."

"The leaves are like an elephant's ears," Sandy said. "Look how big they are. Mrs. Abbott says they're poisonous."

"Dad says so, too." I added.

When ready to harvest, the green stalks ripen to a pinkish-red color. My family liked rhubarb cooked with sugar and used as a sauce over puddings or ice cream. But more often we enjoyed rhubarb pies.

"Sandy, hold a stalk and I'll cut off the leaf, then I'll cut the end of the stalk where it shoots up out of the ground."

"Okay, I'll put them in the basket." Sandy collected them from me.

"I think we have enough for now," Harriet said after a few minutes. "Can you little kids carry your basket?"

"Of course, we can! We're not weaklings," Sandy answered.

After the stalks were rinsed, the rhubarb went through our little guillotine. The guillotine, a chopper, was most often used to slice green beans, wax beans, and apples. It contained a large knife attached to a flat piece of hardwood. Stack, slide, cut! Stack, slide, cut! Stack, slide, cut! We took turns cutting with the guillotine, a favorite task after we had lined up the rhubarb on the wooden cutting board.

"Listen to that beat! Rata tat tat! Rata tat tat! Rata tat tat!" Sandy sang and marched around the kitchen, her hands moving back and forth rapidly. "It sounds like soldiers marching across a wooden floor or a steel bridge."

Even though Raymond was just fifteen, he was our family's main baker. He mixed his piecrust with diligence. To the rhubarb, he added a little vanilla flavoring and lots of sugar.

"You little kids ate all the strawberries we picked and

none are left for my pies. Don't you know Gene likes strawberries with rhubarb pie?" he complained.

The top piecrust was Raymond's drawing board.

"Here's a little diamond for each of us." Ray cut out little diamonds on the dough.

Just as Raymond predicted, when baked and out of the oven the crust was crispy, brown, and juicy.

"Look at that! They're as pretty as a picture! They're too beautiful to eat!" Raymond boasted as he admired his finished product. "These are my creations and my gift to this hungry family!"

"Raymond is the best baker we have. Everything he makes tastes as if it came from a real bakery. Gene isn't crazy about sweet desserts but he likes Raymond's pies," Clarence said that day at supper.

"You can bet on it! Raymond's pies are the best!" Gene savored each forkful.

One pie was gone after one meal and the second pie was on its way. Vanished. There were nine of us when everyone was home and Gene was home on a leave. He had been away for two years. He was stationed at the US Army base in San Francisco, California. When Aunt Almira, Dad's sister, lived with us there were ten. Sometimes she stayed at her own house or at a special hospital.

Gene had come home one other time, too. On his first leave he had ridden with army buddies from San Francisco to Cleveland. From Cleveland he had hopped on a bus and traveled as far east as Albany, New York. Then, he climbed aboard another bus that brought him to Vermont. He hitchhiked the last few miles. I had watched for him as he walked down the hill toward home and I ran to greet him. His duffle bag had been slung over one shoulder. He messed up my hair just as Dad always did.

On his second trip home he drove his own car, a white Ford sedan. On both trips he looked taller than ever. He was thin and his army uniform accentuated his height.

"Son, you're as slender as a fence post," Dad had said to him.

On the last day of school in June, Gene picked us up in his car. His leave was nearly over. He'd be on his way early the next morning. I scrambled to get the front seat.

"Hop in," he said. "Hey! Did everyone pass?"

"I did and I'll be in the fourth grade in September. Johnny passed, too." Sandy sounded relieved.

"I passed and I'm going upstairs into the sixth grade, Gene. Everybody in my class passed, even Bobby."

"I'll be in the seventh grade. Pat and I will be in the same classroom," Carolyn answered.

"And I'm going to high school. Raymond says not to worry about a thing. He'll look after me if I have any trouble," Harriet answered.

"What kind of trouble could you get into?" Gene asked. "There's nothing to worry about."

"I don't know. He thinks I might need his help for something, I guess. He's popular and says no one bothers him."

Earlier in the week, Gene had said to me, "I'm going to stay in California when I finish my three years with the army, Pat. I have one more year to go. I don't want to run the farm. Farming is not for me. This week I worked for Bernie Langevin spreading manure. I won't spend the rest of my life doing that!"

"Oh," is all I managed to say but my heart sank at his news.

"I'll get a job and go to night school. I'll make my living earning a lot more money doing some other kind of work. I have a girlfriend in San Francisco. Maybe I'll get married someday."

"Oh," is all I could say.

I had a lost feeling for a long time when I thought about Gene's plans. I didn't know if I'd ever see him again. California seemed so far away, clear across the USA. We had played catch with his baseball and gloves. Gene taught me how to throw a baseball really fast, too. He was a great fan of the Brooklyn Dodgers.

"Wait and see, Pat. They're going to win the World Series this year or next. I guarantee it. Have you listened

Gene's high school graduation photo

to the games on the radio?"

He shared his sports magazines and baseball cards with me. Cards of Jackie Robinson, Pee Wee Reese, Duke Snider, and Roy Campanella were his favorites. Roy Campanella was my brother's hero and he had been voted the MVP last year. Campanella had said, "I hope to play baseball for as long as I live."

"Jackie Robinson is the first Negro to play baseball in the National League, Pat. He and Campanella are showing everybody that they can play baseball as well as the white players." Jackie Robinson was Gene's other hero.

Although I had seen movies with Negroes and pictures of them I had never seen any in real life. I wondered if they were really different from white people.

After the last supper when Gene had been home and early the next morning, all of Raymond's pies had disappeared except for one large slice.

Gene had stuffed his duffle bag with all of his things including his baseball cards, baseballs, and gloves. His old school lunch pail was filled with some of his favorites including Mom's corned beef sandwiches and Carolyn's chocolate fudge. Packed there, too, was a carefully wrapped slice of pie. His thermos held cold milk.

Before sunrise, my family and I bravely stood at the lawn's edge and waved good-bye to Gene. He, too, waved and he drove out of our driveway on to the dirt road, and west into his future.

We kids were solemn as we called in the cows that morning. Our thoughts remained with the new reality of Gene leaving home for good.

At home that day, we kids went about our chores, ate supper, and engaged in quiet conversation that evening. Raymond practiced his trumpet and Carolyn played the piano. Mom sang to the tunes as they played, her voice resounding throughout the house. Harriet and Sandy played checkers. Dad read his paper. I was playing school with my cut-out figures of kids. Clarence drove off in his Mercury to visit friends. Mostly we were quiet, thinking about Gene.

A few minutes after we girls had gone to bed, there

was a tap on the door. Carolyn and I were reading our magazines. Ray opened the door and tiptoed into the room.

"Gene left behind a couple of old baseball magazines. Do you want them, Pat?"

"Oh, sure, thanks. I'm not sleepy. Thanks, Ray."

"They're yours kiddo. Gene must have forgotten to give them to you. Sweet Dreams."

Chapter 6

CLEARING THE LAND

*The Extension Service is the system of adult education and
vocational training in agriculture maintained jointly
by the federal government and the states.*
A. Whitney Griswold

"There's no time like the present," Dad said when he had made a decision. "We'll get started now. Our crops are doing well. Most of the weeding is done. We'll need everyone's hands for this project."

"I've called Mr. Jameway and he can work for us whenever we need the bulldozer," Clarence added. "I'll call him again and ask him to come over in three days. That's about how long it will take to clear the land of trees and brush."

"We need many hands and Gene isn't here to help. But if we all tackle the project that will be enough time."

"All right then, I'll call him right now and ask him to be here on Monday."

Dad nodded and finished his breakfast. "We'll have our oat crop come September. Oats are one of the fastest growing grains."

Dad had decided to clear about ten acres of land to grow oats, a grain for our dairy cows. Clearing the land was a huge project tucked into Dad's schedule as soon as the crops were growing well. Nearly one hundred years had gone by since the land had been used. Back then, in the

At one time, sheep dominated Vermont farms

19th century, sheep had been brought to Vermont. That same parcel had been cleared and used as a grazing area for sheep.

When Dad cleared the land in 1954, it looked quite different from the way it was when sheep fed on the growing grasses. Now, the sloping ten acres were partially swampy. Other parts were covered with brush, grass, saplings, wildflowers, and weeds like the pesky burdocks and thistles. Evergreens, especially pines and cedars, had sprung to life there along with oak, beech, poplar, and maple.

A rough road, more of a trail really, was visible where the tractor made its annual treks with the gathering tank during the maple sugaring season. Dead tree trunks littered the area, having lost their foothold during ice storms or strong winds. Large boulders and rocks were scattered here and there.

"Previous owners were sheep farmers. That's why we have rock fences all around." Dad pointed toward the old stone fence.

"How do you know that sheep lived here? How do you know about the rocks?" I asked.

"I've checked the land records in Randolph. Rock fences didn't need to be very high because sheep cannot climb as easily as goats. Sheep are content to stay in an enclosed area if they have enough food and water. Wool was cash, money in hand for farmers. The price of wool during the Civil War was forty cents a pound. When times were bad, sheep farmers received maybe fifteen cents a pound."

"How many sheep were in Vermont?" I asked.

"In Randolph, there were as many as eighteen thousand sheep. Most flocks numbered about a hundred but there were thousands of sheep all over Vermont."

"Where was the barn for the sheep?"

"You're full of questions today, Pat. Sheep don't need an enclosed barn like cows and horses. Remember, a sheep's fleece grows to keep it warm. Cold weather helps the fleece grow thick and long. A shed is about all a sheep needs. A sheep farmer owned a dog to protect the sheep from predators. Some sheep owners had pens to keep them safe."

"You know a lot about sheep. How do you know so much?"

"Well, Patty, you're always learning something. Because

I'm older doesn't mean that I've stopped learning. You'll see. There's something to learn every day if you pay attention."

To begin clearing the land, Clarence got out his chainsaw and cut off the limbs of trees that had fallen and lay helter-skelter all around, most of it too rotten for use. But the debris had to be removed. Clarence used a giant chain snuggled around the wood and skidded the mess away with the tractor.

Next, Clarence cut down the largest trees. The maples, oaks, pines, and cedars soon lay on the ground. He cut off the branches leaving only the trunks. He used the tractor with the same chain and skidded each log to a knoll. From there, the logs were rolled on to our truck. Dad took the logs to Webster's sawmill where they were cut up and sold for lumber. The cedar was used for shingles and the pine, maple, and oak were used for furniture or other building needs.

Great sounds were heard all around: the noisy chainsaw, the crashing and crunching as the trees fell to the ground, and the truck's roar when Dad started it.

The larger branches were cut into lengths of about two feet and stacked on the wagon. In some places, we kids carried the wood a long distance before we reached the wagon. It was hard work. It was hot! On this hot day, Kool-Aid was no help.

"I hate this job!" Raymond said time after time. "I'll never do this again in my life! I can't breathe! I can't work this hard in the sun!"

Clarence climbed onto the tractor to pull the wagon to our woodshed. "Okay kids, let's stack this wood neatly. I don't want to have any wood falling on my car." Clarence stored his car in the shed during the winter months.

Back on the land, we dragged the small branches, shrubs, and brush, piling it around the perimeter of the area. Cottontail rabbits could find a safe home under all that brush. No fox, no matter how cunning, could catch them. They could safely nibble the little tender twigs for food.

Sandy joked, "What will the bunnies do for a home when they've eaten all those twigs, Patty?"

The skinny cedar trees were cut with Clarence's noisy chainsaw. The branches were removed and the thin trunks were cut into lengths of six or seven feet and piled on the wagon.

When Dad returned from the sawmill after a few trips, he used an ax to chip one end of each cedar post until it was as pointed as a sharpened pencil.

"Dad said to put these posts all around the edge of the cleared land. Leave space between each one," Raymond complained.

"How much space?" asked Harriet.

"I don't know everything, ask Dad."Raymond waited for Dad to answer.

"Leave four or five in a pile about every thirty feet."

"I don't know how much thirty feet is. How long is that?"

Harriet was puzzled.

"Leave them in a few piles and we'll figure the distance later. Okay, you little kids help, too," Dad said.

And so the posts were piled here and there along the edge of the developing land. They had a special use as fence posts to keep the cows out of the soon-to-be-planted oat field.

Finally, after three days of work, it was Mr. Jameway's turn. When he arrived in his truck, he started up the machine and backed the noisy bulldozer down the truck's ramp onto the ground.

At once, Mr. Jameway surveyed the area and got right to work. His bulldozer seemed to defy gravity as it noisily rumbled around and tilted in one direction and then in the other. Over time, rocks had found their way to the surface, pushed up by the freezing and thawing of the land. He selected rocks, lowered the bucket loader, captured the rocks, and dumped them at the edge of the land. Next, he attached a chain to each stump and the bulldozer strained, groaned, and pulled it up, roots and all. Every stump was taken to the edges of the developing field just like the boulders. Later, Clarence cut the stumps into manageable sizes. They would provide fuel for our sugarhouse.

What noises! The dozer groaned and grunted its way across the field, the stones crashed and clanked against each other as they were lifted, moved, and dropped by the dozer's bucket loader.

The dozer leveled out the soil. Using his bucket loader, Mr. Jameway dug a trench on the wet side creating a ditch for water drainage. Sometimes the dozer's tracks spun in the swampy area making great whizzing sounds. Dad worried that the bulldozer would get stuck, or worse, fall over on its side as one track tipped and sank more than the other.

"Be careful! You're leaning too much to the right," Dad shouted as the machine's tracks churned along and gave the operator a lopsided ride.

Mr. Jameway nodded, waved his arm, and tipped his hat as if in a dance with his machine. Using the bucket loader, he leveled the land of many of its hollows formed by the boulders and the trees' roots.

"He looks like a cowboy on a horse," shouted Sandy as we watched him.

I nodded, "He's the Lone Ranger. Hi ho Silver!"

Occasionally, Mr. Jameway stood up on the moving bulldozer to get a better view of his surroundings. He gazed this way and that way making decisions about which rock or stump needed removal next. He rested occasionally, put the dozer in neutral, dug a handkerchief from his pocket, and wiped sweat from his face. He stood, stretched his arms, sipped a cold drink from a jug he carried on the bulldozer's floor, and gazed skyward squinting into the sun.

"It's a hot day," he remarked to my father.

"It's nearly ninety degrees. It'll be hotter before the day is done. This humidity doesn't help," my dad agreed.

An example of a boulder left by a glacier...too big to move!

After a while the land was as level as it could be. Mr. Farr, the county agent from the Extension Office in Chelsea, stopped by. "How's the project going?"

"You can see that we're making progress." Dad laughed. "Many hands make light work."

"You're the pioneers on this land. You're making cultivatable acreage. You're improving the value of your farm with this project."

Mr. Farr spoke about soil conservation, erosion, and water runoff. Dad nodded in agreement with everything Mr. Farr talked about. He and Clarence relied on him for the best information about land use for our crops and the best care of our dairy cows.

"With your large meadow just west of your house and this cleared space, you have flat, tillable acreage other farmers around here only dream about," Mr. Farr said.

"We've put in an honest day's work," Dad grinned.

With all the bulldozer work complete, Dad paid Mr. Jameway for his services. They shook hands. Dad guided Mr. Jameway as he drove the machine up the ramp and on to his truck. Soon he'd be headed home, but first Clarence stopped his work to ask him a few questions.

Clarence had admired the work of the bulldozer. "How much does a bulldozer cost? How much diesel fuel does it use? What is the cost of diesel fuel? Do farms get a break on the diesel fuel tax? What is its horsepower? Where did you buy it?"

Mr. Jameway patiently answered all of Clarence's questions. He showed him the motor.

"Thanks for the information." Clarence shook hands with him.

Clarence plowed up the grassy sod that remained on the new field. He shouted to Dad, "This soil is black and fertile. But there are still plenty of rocks peeking up through the soil. We'll have to move them."

Dad grinned, waved, and signaled two thumbs up.

As Clarence plowed more rocks appeared. Some were a hefty size. Dad cringed when he heard the plow's blade squeal as it made contact with a big rock. A squeal and a crunching sound ensured that the steel plow was in trouble. When the plow's sharp edge hit a big rock, it broke off just like ribbon candy snapped apart by hungry kids at

Christmas time.

And so, a couple of times, Dad drove to the house and used the telephone to call the welder, who soon arrived and fixed our broken plow.

The plow was constructed of strong, sturdy steel, so you can imagine the size of a rock that could break a plow. The welder put the plow together again with a special steel rod heated to the melting point. He used a flame from a torch attached to a small fuel tank. To protect himself, he wore special goggles and a metal shield covering his face. As the molten metal hardened, it adhered one part to the other. Clarence talked with the welder for a long time.

After a time, the plow had completed its job on the field. Everything looked A-okay! Except…now the hard work began. The rocks had to be removed before the land could be harrowed and seeded with oats. What a job!

"I hate this job! Who can stand this?" Raymond's allergies continued to bother him especially now due to the humidity and high temperature.

"What's the matter, Raymee? We're the pioneers on this land. Feel happy about it," Sandy teased.

We four sisters knew Raymond suffered with his breathing problems.

"Imagine what it must be like to not get enough air in your lungs. He wheezes and coughs a lot and can't get his breath." Carolyn sounded sympathetic.

We all nodded and Sandy added, "I feel like that after I've

run for a long time, don't you?"

We all continued to gather the rocks and throw them on to the wagon. Stones were lifted with a struggle, others with sheer willpower.

When finally the wagon was full, Clarence drove to the ditch Mr. Jameway had created. We kids threw a layer of rocks at its base. That would prevent the ditch from becoming a deep gully because the water could run off better and not build little pools.

Then Clarence took off for the end of the field nearest to the road. He had built a motorized lift on the wagon. Now, he released it and most of the remaining rocks were dumped and formed a pile which grew and grew. If anybody wanted rocks for their lawn or for their home, they could drive over and select their favorites. They were free! Over the years, people had taken rocks from the old stone fence and the piles near the road.

"The rock piles have grown again," Dad complained. "People can have all the rocks they can carry away!"

"Where do all of these rocks come from?" Sandy asked. "I've never seen so many rocks. How did they get here?"

"I know," I answered. "The glaciers left them. Millions of years ago, this land was covered by glaciers."

"But how did they get here?"

"Glaciers began with snow that did not melt for a long, long time. More and more snow fell. And because it was so cold it snowed year round. The heavy snow pressed down on the snow underneath for thousands of layers. The glaciers inched along very slowly. Very slowly! They picked up passengers like boulders, rocky mountaintops, gravel, and other stuff.

"Over time, the temperatures changed and it warmed up. Giant heavy pieces of the glacier fell away that carried boulders and rocks. As a glacier melted, lakes were formed in the depressed areas. Rocks were left helter-skelter and whenever you see large boulders or rocks, they were probably left by glaciers."

"How do you know so much about glaciers? Where did you learn all that old stuff?"

"Sandy, I am a lot older than you, two years older. When you are older you'll learn about those things. Mrs. Abbott told us all about the glaciers in science class." Here's a joke about glaciers.

Student to teacher: "What happened to the glaciers? Where did they go?"

Teacher to student: "The glaciers have gone back for more rocks. When they return, there will be more rocks to remove."

"Now, we need to help Daddy build the fence. The grass is always greener on the other side of the fence," Sandy laughed.

"Yes, and this time the greener grass will be the field of oats!" I replied.

Chapter 7

NOT YOUR ORDINARY OATS

*If you want the rainbow, you've got to put
up with a little rain.*
Dolly Parton

"All you kids have done a good job of distributing these cedar posts around the field," Dad said as he began building the fence around it.

With the post-hole digger, Dad dug holes about a foot deep into the ground and eight to ten feet apart. He used the heavy sledgehammer and forced a post into each hole.

Once in a while, Dad received a sudden jolt. He grimaced, rubbed his sore arm, and groaned, "There's a rock under here. I can't go deep enough in this spot. I'll have to start a new hole."

Finally, Dad used u-shaped nails and barbed wire to build the fence. With a hammer, he pounded a nail into a cedar post with a strand of barbed wire forced against the post. The task took a long time, almost all day.

Each fence post held four rows of the sharp barbed wire placed evenly apart like a musical staff. "This fence is built to last. The tight barbed wires will prevent any curious cow from squeezing through it," Dad bragged.

Hundreds of feet of barbed wire were purchased, coiled

An old stone fence marks the boundary between two farms

on a cylindrical column. I rolled the wire along with my foot. Sandy helped by going to the next cedar post pile and handed one to Dad as he finished a new hole. With our feet, we both tamped the dirt nice and tight around each post. After a few posts were in the ground, Dad added wire to them, using clippers to cut the wire when necessary.

"Be careful, Pat. The barbs are nasty and can cut your fingers or your leg. Barbed wire can go right through your gloves and work clothes."

"All right, Dad." I paid attention as we moved from fence post to fence post.

"Here's another cedar post, Daddy," Sandy spoke as we worked together.

Clarence spread fertilizer and manure on the new field. He used the harrow to mix the manure and the fertilizer into the soil, and to break up sod in the same way that he had prepared our garden and vegetable fields.

Occasionally, one of the harrow's disks clanged against a pesky rock hidden in the soil. My dad cringed. "Oh, no! We can't be calling the welder. Not again!"

The clanging sounds continued. One or two disks were nicked, and some damage was done but not seriously enough to call the welder.

"That's one less thing to worry about. Hiring the welder has been expensive. I know he has a family with children to feed and clothe, but he charges too much," Dad fumed as he continued his fence-building project.

Clarence had ideas about becoming a welder. He had talked with the welder when he had repaired the broken plow's sharp edge a couple days earlier.

"The equipment will pay for itself and we can make extra money for other things we need around here. Every time we call the welder it's money down the drain. Plus, I can hire myself out and do welding jobs for others."

"I'll think about it."

When Dad ended a conversation like that, it was pretty much a done deal. Clarence knew that and so would wait patiently for Dad's decision.

When finally the fence was finished, my father said to no one in particular, "There, that job is done. Now we can worry about getting other things done."

Sandy and I looked at each other. We knew Dad was old-fashioned, and he repeated some thoughts again and again. We grinned and poked each other in the arm. We also knew Dad was older, a lot older, than most Dads we knew.

Sandy and I helped Dad put the remaining cedar posts on the truck. Dad collected the remaining wire.

Clarence had other ideas about fencing. "We don't need any more cedar posts. I know this field is too far from the barn to connect the electricity. But we should connect the pastures near the barn to electricity with simple wire and metal posts. Cows will touch an electric fence only once. The shock will make them shy away from the fence. When the fence is in, it's there to stay." That was something else Dad was thinking about.

You may be wondering about the value of oats and whether or not people eat them. They do. When ripened, the oats are rolled or flattened by big machines. Some kinds of breads and cereals contain oats. Cheerios had been around since Harriet was a baby.

Dad said, "People have eaten oatmeal since time began. Oatmeal fills an empty belly."

The next day, Clarence planted the field with oat seeds, a kind of tall grass. He drove the tractor as the seeder spread the seeds behind it in a great, wide swath like a gigantic fan. Sandy, Dad, and I watched Clarence's progress. Dad hoped for rain.

"Rain will help the seeds germinate, take root, and grow. We are producing some of our own grain for our animals and won't have to buy as much," Dad declared.

"How much does it cost to buy grain? This is a lot of work for just cow grain," I grumbled as I was tired.

"Grain costs too much. This field will be useful every year for some crop or other. We'll get ahead this way. It's a lot of work, that's for sure. Idle people have the least leisure."

As Dad, Sandy, and I began our walk back to our house, he looked toward the sky and said, "Let it rain. Now! We need the rain!"

"Sandy can you do a rain dance?" I kidded. Sandy danced along the path, steps ahead of Dad and me.

Dad looked again at the sky, "It's hot, it's humid, and I think the clouds are darkening. That means rain! We need a nice steady rain, not a sudden burst from the sky." Dad whistled and messed up my hair.

Raymond had prepared scarecrows. They were set out in our fields to scare away the crows and other birds that could ruin a crop by eating the seeds before they had a chance to germinate. And crows liked to fly in and eat young squash or other visible vegetables maturing in the fields or in our garden. Ray's scarecrows stood in our garden and in our potato and squash fields.

Ray looked at us kids, "I need ONE helper today for

this job. I'll plant the two scarecrows in the oat field today."

"I'll help you," Harriet offered. "We'll need a hammer or something to pound them into the earth."

"Oh, yeah, I'll borrow one from Clarence's toolbox." Soon the two were on their way, each carrying a scarecrow. Ray's scarecrows were works of art.

At supper that day, Raymond joked, "I've made five scarecrows this summer. The others were too old to use anymore. No bird will dare to get close to my designs because they look just like you little kids!"

"Oh, Raymee, you say that all the time! How many times are you going to tell Patty and me that we look like your BEAUTIFUL scarecrows?" asked Sandy.

Raymond laughed.

Soon the oats began to grow. At first they looked like a field of dark green, stubby grass. In a short while, the stalks grew over four feet high and light green. The stalks seemed to salute the sun as they swayed with the breeze.

Late in the summer, the oats would be amber in color, ripened, and ready for harvest. The seeds would weigh just enough to cause the stalks to bend slightly without any wind. This reminded me of the song, "America the Beautiful" that we sang at school.

> *Oh, beautiful for spacious skies,*
> *For amber waves of grain...*

America! America!
God shed his grace on thee."

"Before they're completely ready for harvest, we have many other tasks to complete around here. Thank God there have been no strong winds or nasty thunderstorms. The oats are tall, and soon will be top heavy, and the stalks could break if the winds are too strong," Dad fretted.

Chapter 8

THE BUSYNESS OF BEES

The highest and best form of efficiency is the
spontaneous cooperation of a free people.
Woodrow Wilson

Dad's prayers were answered. The rain came and helped our oats get a good start. It was 1954.

I understood many of the things Dad talked about when he visited with neighbors and friends. Often Dad reminded me, "You're eleven now. Use your brain, Pat. That's as important as using your hands for work."

"One hand washes the other," Dad stated enthusiastically after he reached an agreement with someone. "Two wrongs don't make a right," he'd admonish us when in error. "More people know Tom Fool than Tom Fool knows" was one of his favorites. "You're the apple of my eye" and "You're the salt of the earth" were highly sought-after compliments. "We'll cross that bridge when we get to it," was another phrase he used when he wasn't quite ready to make a decision.

Mr. Langevin farmed on land next to ours. He owned dairy cows and grew vegetables for himself and his family. His immediate family consisted of only his sister, Lucille.

During one of his frequent visits to our home, he said

to Dad, "I am French, from family many brothers and sisters in Quebec. I go see two times a year. Lucille go aussi [also]." Mr. Langevin motioned with his hands as if driving his old, noisy truck. "We drive all day. Yes?"

Dad nodded his understanding. "Oui, [Yes] I see."

Later, Dad told us how Mr. Langevin and his sister could easily leave their farm. I had asked Dad, "How can they leave their cows? Who takes care of them? Who feeds his horses? When can we go somewhere?"

"Who does all his work when he's gone?" asked Sandy. "Who milks his cows two times a day? And, who feeds them? Hey, when are we going to go somewhere?"

Ignoring most of our questions, Dad told us that Bernie and Lucille knew many people.

"There are other farmers all around the Randolph area, mostly Catholics, who have relatives in Quebec. Most of them were born there and they speak French. They moved here to have their own farms. They're all friends. They pitch in and help one another."

I had three classmates at school who spoke French at home. I decided to ask Bernard Bean, Florien Vogel, and Ferdinand La Rock if they knew Bernie Langevin and his sister Lucille. School was out for the summer, but I'd see them in town on the Fourth of July.

In addition to his vegetable garden and dairy cows, Mr. Langevin had one special cash crop: honey. He tended the bees in his numerous beehives. Not one of us dared to go near them. We had learned not to mess around with bees, wasps, or hornets.

"You stay 'way from beehives! Stay 'way! No go near," Mr. Langevin warned. He motioned to his row of beehives along the stone fence that served as the boundary between the two farms. "No good go near! Stay 'way!"

Sandy and I nodded to demonstrate our complete agreement. Mr. Langevin was serious, not his usual jolly self when he spoke about bees. He knew that bees could become dangerous if disturbed by us. The bees, in turn, would be dangerous with him or anyone else. Dad had warned all of us about the dangers of wild beehives, too. Dad had given permission to another neighbor to collect honey from a colony of bees that had built a hive in an old tree trunk near our sugarhouse.

"He can have all the honey he dares to take," Dad had said with a chuckle. "As for me I'm not going near that old tree filled with swarming bees. You little kids stay away, too."

Mr. Langevin spoke French very well but had a little trouble with English. During one of his visits with my dad, he asked if he could place beehives in the fields at the farthest boundary of our farms. "My bees get more blossoms, make more honey." Dad agreed that it was a good idea.

All kinds of wildflowers grew around our farm. Morning glories climbed high on whatever growth was nearby

Queen Ann's Lace

with blossoms of pink, blue, lavender, and white. Daisies, brown-eyed Susans, bright yellow buttercups, a deep yellow goldenrod, and colorful cosmos grew in our fields, meadows, and along our buildings. Delicate Queen Anne's lace, white in color, grew on tall stems swaying with any summer breeze that came along. Wild purple asters and paintbrushes of orange, red, and yellow bloomed in our pastures. Bushy bridal spirea and lilacs bloomed on our lawn along the road's edge.

Dad often said, with a flourish of one arm or another, "From spring until the first autumn frost, some kinds of flowers are in bloom. The bees are busy."

Even though Aunt Almira, Dad's sister, disapproved, in early spring, we prepared a green salad with fresh

Red clover, Vermont's state flower

dandelions adding vinegar, oil, and salt. "You children will get sick if they're not cooked," she warned.

Early settlers in Vermont enjoyed dandelions after a long cold winter of root vegetables and smoked or salted meats. Fresh vegetables, then as now, were favorites.

"People from town like our dandelions because they make dandelion wine. I need to find a recipe and make some wine," Raymond said.

Dad replied, "No one needs to be making wine in this family and least of all a fifteen-year-old boy!"

Dad was against the overuse of alcohol. Sometimes he sipped from his stash of sap beer savored by visitors and customers. He and Uncle Jim produced sap beer after the maple sugaring season ended each spring.

On special occasions, they sipped from their bottles of homebrew. That's all the alcohol that was in our home.

Our fields of red clover produced forage for the animals and nectar for the honeybees. Sometimes on a hot day, I could hear the honeybees at work as each moved from one clover blossom to another. Buzz! Buzz! Buzz.

Have I mentioned the potato blossoms? They formed beautiful white blossoms on leafy green stems. And never forget the many squash blossoms. The squash blossoms were a deep, deep yellow. "Like popsicles! They're the color of orange popsicles," Sandy exclaimed.

As soon as our vegetable garden sprang to life, bees found pea blossoms, green bean blossoms, yellow tomato blossoms and others for their nectar gathering.

On one visit, Mr. Langevin showed us a honeycomb he had brought with him. "The bees build waxy honeycombs in beehive, oui? They keep honey there. I get a lot, I give you a little." He repeated, "I get a lot, I give you a little."

Bernie grinned and motioned with his hands to show how much a lot was and how much a little was. My father nodded and motioned with his hands to show that he had understood. The deal was sealed.

Sandy and I giggled when we heard Mr. Langevin say, "I get a lot, I give you a little." Dad chuckled, too. That was good because Dad was a worrier. Dad and Uncle Jim worried about spending too much money on taxes and grain for our animals. Father worried about his sister, Aunt Almira, who was often ill, and sometimes lived with us. So his laughter was a good sign.

Dad warned us to be careful wherever we were. "Wild honeybees will find an old tree trunk or a stable area to make a home. Sometimes they'll build a hive in the woods using old leaves as a base. You could step on one."

"What do they look like?" Sandy asked.

"That's the problem, Sweety. The nests look like the leaves. They're hard to see. Be careful."

Mr. Langevin built special boxes to attract colonies of bees. A man-made beehive is a boxlike rectangular tower, perhaps three feet tall when stacked, and as wide as two feet. Inside, the colony builds waxy honeycombs on screen-like slats. They live inside and store honey, their food source. As they produce honey, it gradually builds up in the layers of the combs.

One well-cared-for hive can produce many, many pounds of honey each year. Honeybees are the only insects that produce food for people. There is a lot to know about bees and beehives as there is with any topic.

Later in the season, on a hot summer day, Mr. Langevin's truck rumbled into our driveway and came to a sudden, stuttering stop. Mr. Langevin opened its squeaky door, hopped down from the cab, reached into the back of the truck for a large metal container, and carried it into our house. He was delivering the honey still in the honeycombs. His honeycombs were stacked on a metal sheet about the size of a cookie sheet but much deeper. I noticed bees' wings and other bee parts embedded in the honeycombs.

"*Bonjour*! [Hello!]" Bernie carefully set the honey and then his black felt hat on the kitchen table. Dad and Bernie began to talk.

Mr. Langevin's curly black hair matched his black whiskers. Because of his hat and beard, Raymond liked to call him Mr. Pilgrim, but never to his face.

Immediately my mother removed the honeycombs and placed them into empty cake pans. Deep golden honey slowly oozed out of them. Sandy and I cut off waxy pieces and popped them into our mouths. Honey dripped down our chins. Our hands grew sticky. Sandy and I licked our fingers free of the stickiness. So sticky!

"Oh, Sandy! This honey and the honeycomb taste like the sweetest gum I've ever had!"

"Yuck! Now it tastes waxy and crumbly." Sandy spat the tasteless mess into the wastebasket and I soon followed.

"Save some of that honey for cooking." Mom reached for a strainer, poured honey into it, and thus removed the multiple bee and waxy parts. She worked at that task for a long while. "This is sticky! So sticky, Bernie!" Mom said between sighs several times.

When finished, Mom emptied and rinsed Mr. Langevin's containers and returned them to him. "Here you are, Bernie."

"*Merci* [Thank you]," he murmured. "Is stuki, [sticky] yes?"

"Oui! Stuki!" Mom smiled, arched her eyebrows, and nodded.

Mr. Langevin seemed amused and glanced at us often as Sandy and I devoured the honey. He and my dad discussed the weather as it related to their farm crops.

"*Merci* for the honey, Bernie." Dad chuckled. "You can see that sweets don't last long around here."

"Got to go, too many bridges to cross." Bernie stood and donned his hat.

"Oh, let me tell you about the project. Sit down, Bernie. We've planted oats for the animals." Dad could be long-winded and this was a time. Bernie sat down again and removed his hat.

Eventually, Bernie said, "Life one thing upon another. I got to go."

"Thanks again. We'll put the honey to good use. I'll let you know about our oat crop as it ripens."

Mr. Langevin put on his hat and left our house. He hopped into his truck, started it up, and roared off in the direction of his home. He traveled through our pasture on a road only slightly visible to the naked eye. At one time, this old road had been a part of the Boston to

Montreal stage or post road.

At their home, Lucille strained the honey to take out any pieces of the honeycomb and bee parts. She poured the strained honey into jars of different sizes. She wrote HONEY on each label and the year it was processed. And she drew a pretty little clover blossom and colored it a deep pink. She drew a wavy black outline all around the edges of each label. Lucille owned a big box of Crayola crayons. The black and pink colors were almost used up. People traveled to the Langevin home to buy the honey. Honey was their cash crop.

Dad had said that Bernie Langevin was a good neighbor and a man of his word. My father tapped Mr. Langevin's maple trees in the springtime. My father jokingly declared, "I get a lot, I give a little to Bernie! One hand washes the other."

Chapter 9

CALLING IN THE COWS

Does the road wind uphill all the way?
Yes, to the very end.
Will the day's journey take the whole long day?
From morn to night, my friend.
Christina G. Rossetti

"Come, bossy! Come bossy!" My sisters and I called in unison. We girls, Lassie, and sometimes Raymond, called in the cows from the pasture twice a day. Their udders were full, they wanted to be milked, and they anticipated their ration of grain. "Come, bossy!" They headed toward the barn.

Some mornings, the fog had rolled in over the hills. Sandy and I loved to walk through the fog. In the distance, the cows looked ghostlike. "Hold my hand, Patty! I'm afraid I'll get lost in this fog."

"Not a chance," I'd answer. "The fog will lift as soon as it's daybreak. We'll frighten away the ghosts with Lassie's help. Look at the barn. It barely shows through the fog. It looks like an unfinished painting."

"What? I don't see it."

"Look at the fog and..."

"Oh, yeah, you're right Patty. The canvas is the fog and the part of the barn we see is the beginning of a painting. I get it now. And our house hasn't even been started yet."

Other mornings, if we didn't wear our raingear, we would be soaked. We'd find the cows getting a little shelter from the canopy of leaves provided by our oaks and maples. "Look, Pat, we're their alarm clocks. They're still asleep. The cows don't like the rain anymore than we do."

"Yeah, they know we're coming, Sandy. They want to get inside the barn as soon as they can."

During those rainy mornings, Lassie stopped at the old horse barn. She waited there and seemed to say, "I'm not getting drenched. You go ahead and get the cows by yourselves this morning. I'll stay nice and dry waiting here for you."

Other mornings were picture perfect, a scene right from *Vermont Life.* In early summer, the rich greens showed in the grasses, the leaves, and new growth on the evergreens. Other times, the dew on the ground sparkled as the first rays of sun peaked over the horizon.

In the autumn, our footsteps crunched through the frost on the ground and anyone with eyes couldn't help but notice the multi-colored leaves of the maples, oaks, and sumacs. The pinecones, in contrast to the green needles, were turning a deep, deep brown and falling to the ground.

"Calling in the cows" may be unfamiliar to someone

who hasn't spent time on a farm. During late spring, all summer, and into the fall, our dairy cows lived outdoors in the pastures. They were brought from the pasture to the barn early in the morning and again late in the afternoon to be milked.

When it was wintertime, the cows lived in the barn. They lumbered outside into the barnyard area for a few minutes of exercise, sunshine, and fresh water from the tub every day. Occasionally, the weather turned less frigid. This change in the temperature was a great treat for our animals.

"Look at the cows, Patty! Look at them dancing and prancing around! They must be happy today!" Sandy pointed first at Cassie and then at Bertha.

"Dad says they like the warmer weather and they like to run around when it isn't too cold," I explained. "Dad says they don't have a care in the world, but I know they care about their calves."

"Yes, and they like their grain and molasses so they must care about that," answered Sandy. I nodded.

During summer, the cows ate grass in the pastures and drank water from the brook that wound through part of the pastureland. If it was very, very hot, the cows cooled off by standing in the brook. They chewed their cuds and swished the flies from their backsides with long bushy tails. With closed eyes, they looked very content as if that was the best thing in the world to do.

Other times they spent a hot, lazy afternoon in the shade of the large maple and oak trees that lined the pasture. Once in a while they would lie down to be more comfortable.

Dad, Mom, and Clarence were the earliest risers in the family. Mother prepared breakfast and if it was a bread-baking day, she mixed the dough and let the yeast begin its job.

"Let's get started," Dad said. "It's time to start another day of milking and getting the cows' grain ready." He and Clarence headed for the barn.

About 6 am, Mom called from the bottom of the stairs, "Harriet, Carolyn, Pat, and Sandy." And sometimes Raymond. "It's time to be up." We tumbled from our beds. We hurriedly dressed, sprang fully awake as we hurried down the stairs, and left the house in pursuit of the cows.

"Come bossy, come bossy," we called as we headed for the pastures. "Come bossy, come bossy."

Lassie stayed near our side but darted off after the cows as soon as she spied them.

Sometimes, though, Lassie became sidetracked and would run off in pursuit of a rabbit or a squirrel in the nearby woodland. The squirrel would escape and run up a tree trunk. The cottontail rabbit would race to the edge of the woods. There the cottontail hid in its home of brush, shrubs, and tall grasses. During all my days of completing this chore of calling in the cows, I never witnessed Lassie catching a squirrel or a cottontail rabbit. "Give it up, Lassie. They're too fast for you!" I'd say.

When Lassie was attentive, she barked and herded the cows toward the barn. Usually, the cows followed the leader and headed toward the barn whether or not Lassie helped. If an occasional cow defied her, Lassie barked and nipped at her heels until she moved along with the others.

"The cows will come to the barn. Cows like to be milked because their udders are full. And they like the grain. If that dog were smarter, she'd bring the cows into the barn without your help. She's the laziest dog I have ever seen," Dad said after he had watched Lassie's antics from the barn.

I felt differently about Lassie than Dad did. I loved my dog. She was my buddy. She was a collie just like Lassie in the book. I also knew that Lassie was the star on a television show.

By 1954, I had watched television only two times in my whole life. Once at a 4-H meeting at Mrs. LaFrance's house we watched a program about white men exploring Africa. They wore army-type uniforms and helmet-shaped hats held on to their heads by a strap that circled under their chins. Each time they spoke or moved their heads slightly their helmets bobbled around. Black boots covered their legs nearly up to their knees.

During the program the explorers were in grave danger. Enemies had heated a gigantic pot of water over a smoky bonfire. The African natives were planning to boil and eat the explorers. Eventually, the explorers woke up. One had been experiencing a bad dream about cannibals. They continued on their journey.

The television was fuzzy, as if being watched through a terrible snowstorm or blizzard. You could not see the action clearly through the haze.

When I told my dad about the program, he retorted, "What a waste of time television is! It's such nonsense!"

"It was scary and I like the television," I had said.

"Pat, television is a waste of time. Tell me, what did you and the other kids accomplish by watching that show?"

"I dunno, but it was scary and sort of exciting."

***

When the cows were taken to our larger pasture, we led them across the road. That meant stopping any traffic that came along. Most people, usually farm families or neighbors, patiently waited for the cows to safely cross. Raymond directed the traffic.

"Slow down! Slow down!" he'd shout with a commanding voice and a raised hand to one or another of our neighbors as they braked their vehicle to make way for the cows.

With great fanfare, Raymond eagerly waved the cars along as soon as the cows had safely crossed the road. He'd bow and with a swoop of one arm, coax people along their way.

"Okay, you can move on now," he'd proclaim.

Strangers in cars stopped to wait as our cows crossed the road. They seemed amused by the temporary chaos of the cows grouped together hurrying across the road. Raymond, outgoing and friendly, chatted, "How do you like this warm weather? Where are you from? Have you read in the newspaper about ....? Do you like jazz? It sounds better than that silly 'doggie' song, don't you think? Have you seen the movie playing in Randolph? Don't you worry, Lassie's bark is worse than her bite. Lassie won't bite your tires," he'd charmingly say as he urged her to be quiet. Or, he'd insist, "Lassie's letting off steam. She won't hurt you. She's as friendly as a kitten with a tummy full of warm milk."

Raymond asked the occasional out-of-towner, "How fast does that car go? What other colors does this model come in? Is it hard to shift the gears? How much does a new one cost? Where could I find a good used one?"

My father said, "Son, you're never short for words. You've got the gift of gab."

Our home was located on a little-used country road at a Y-shaped crossroads between those traveling to East Randolph in one direction and to South Randolph in the opposing direction. The other road climbed a hill west to Randolph Center and then to Randolph. Mostly local people used these dirt roads.

An old path connected at this intersection and led to Mr. Langevin's farm. He and my family were the only people who used that old road heading north. The road passed through our yard, the old apple orchard and pastures, and joined Mr. Langevin's pastureland. It eventually led to his house and beyond to more farmland. Every time the road was used, the fences for both farms needed to be opened and then closed.

One night at supper, Dad told us, "Mr. Langevin's house was an old stagecoach stop. His house was an inn. If you stayed on the stagecoach from start to finish, you'd go from Boston all the way to Montreal."

"What? Mr. Langevin's house was an inn? That old house? Who'd want to stay there?" I asked.

I had been there with my sisters to visit Mr. Langevin's sister, Lucille. She didn't speak much English and Mr. Langevin occasionally asked us to visit to cheer her up.

"She *seule* [lonely]. Come see, come visit," Mr. Langevin had explained. Whenever we visited, Miss Langevin smiled at us.

"You like *pain*, [bread], *oui*?" she asked. She offered us bread she had baked herself and spread it with honey. The honey sweetened the chewy, crusty bread. "Is good, *oui?"*

My sisters and I giggled. *"Oui, merci."*

"That house is falling apart," Carolyn added. "The last time we visited, the porch floor creaked and sagged wherever I stepped. The old screen door has holes in it and it's missing a hinge."

Harriet continued, "The kitchen floor is uneven and the ceiling is so low you can almost touch it with your hand."

"Yes, that's all true. But Bernie's fixing it. Time," Dad replied. "Time," he repeated again. "It's an old house over one hundred fifty years old. He needs time to work on it. Clarence and I will give him a hand this winter."

"Bernie needs a better toolbox," Clarence laughed. "That's falling apart, too."

After the cows were fed, we tended to other tasks. We quickly fed the calves their grain and milk or water. We fed the pigs their mash and any food waste Clarence or Dad had brought with them from the kitchen. We re-filled the pigs' water containers.

When we had finished, we were hungry. We left the barn and ran to the family kitchen where breakfast waited. If Ray had stayed in the kitchen, he had whipped up pop-overs, muffins, pancakes, or best of all fresh apple cider donuts! Or, Mom would have prepared eggs of varying styles with ham, sausage or bacon, or a heaping plate of French toast or hot cereal and milk.

Lassie received her food. There, behind the wood stove sat her food bowl and another bowl for water. She ate mostly table scraps.

On school days, after the ritual of calling in the cows, we kids tidied ourselves, changed into our school clothing, and set off for school with our lunch buckets and books. Full of energy, we hurried along the gravel road and climbed its steep hill. At its top, we passed Brigham's apple orchard and a few paces later passed by the town cemetery. As we approached the school, we greeted our friends who had arrived. If we were early, we enjoyed the teeter-totters or the school swings until the school bell signaled the beginning of another school day.

Summers meant freedom to hop on our bikes and enjoy leisure time until other chores needed our attention.

Chapter 10

ORNERY ANIMALS

Accidents will occur in the best-regulated families.
Charles Dickens

Everyone in the family was worried about Harriet. Would she get better? How serious were her wounds? Would she go to sleep and never wake up? What if she didn't start eating again? Or drinking? Harriet was so ill her appetite had left her. She couldn't get out of bed without Mother's help. Ever since the accident Lassie had stayed close to Harriet.

Sandy was in a dismal condition. She cried and asked, again and again, "When will Harriet be better? What's really wrong with her, Mommy?"

"She needs time to heal, Sandy. Harriet is suffering from her wounds and from trauma. I feel terrible about getting her up every two hours but that's doctor's orders. It's a struggle for her to walk, let alone get up and down the stairs without my help. I hope her wounds are healing. Her stitches are holding." Mom sighed and sat in the chair beside Harriet and Lassie.

Dad had always cautioned, or as Raymond said, preached to never surprise any animal. "Never approach an animal until you have its attention. Animals don't have eyes in the back of their heads. Never walk too close to give one a chance to butt you with their heads or to kick you with a hoof."

"Dad's got a sermon for everything!" Raymond insisted. "Clean your plates. Take all the food you want, but eat it. Don't waste it. Waste not, want not. I get sick of hearing him talk and preach, talk and preach."

Our bull had been dangerous. A long time ago, when I was just a toddler, a bull was common on most dairy farms to ensure herd growth through breeding. Our bull was kept in a special pen in one corner of our barn. No one was allowed near that bull except Dad. When the bull was released from its pen for service, Dad cleared everyone out of the barn.

In my memory of the bull, I hear snorts and bellows from its pen and I see its mammoth size. If the bull had been a fire, a terrible flame-filled area could be seen. That's how scary and fierce looking he appeared. I would peer at him through the steel bars of his cage. His eyes looked furious and he shook his head angrily at me or anyone who was nearby.

Dad would hear the bull's snorts. "Get away from that bull's pen! Don't go anywhere near it!" Dad harshly reminded me.

After Dad sold the bull, he said, "It's a good thing we no longer need a bull. Artificial insemination is the best thing the Extension Service has done for us. I was

Holstein calf soon after birth

always wary of that bull. He was as unpredictable and mean spirited a creature I've ever known. I don't know why some farmers insist on keeping a bull."

Dad told stories of leading the bull with a long pole attached to a ring pierced through its nostrils. The nose ring was placed in its sensitive nostrils to keep the bull under control.

Dad cautioned that cows, too, could be dangerous. "If you frighten a cow, it can turn on you in a split second. Always give a cow time to see you when you approach her." Again, we didn't always listen.

Dad thought we should stay out of the pigpen, too. "The sow will think you mean her piglets harm," he warned. We didn't always listen.

Dad also cautioned us to beware of dogs. "If a dog

doesn't know you, it could attack you. A dog wants to be protective of its master, you know. Stay clear of strange dogs."

You know what Dad and Mr. Langevin thought about us kids going near beehives or hornet nests.

One hot, summer afternoon, Carolyn, Sandy, and I were walking down the sloping, hilly pasture to call in the cows for their late afternoon milking. Lassie tagged along as usual demonstrating her wayward behavior with scents to sniff, small animals to pursue, and a general disregard for the daily task. Suddenly Lassie perked up, her eyes and ears at full attention. She ran quickly toward one of the cows quite a distance from the rest of the herd. Bark! Bark! Her yelp was earnest and serious. Bark! Bark!

"Oh Lassie, for Pete's sake, simmer down! Haven't you ever seen a cow with a newborn calf?" asked Sandy.

The only Guernsey we owned had calved. She was a nice enough cow but for some reason we had never given her a name.

"Come, Lassie!" I yelled. "Don't scare the little calf." I could see that the newborn was standing on wobbly, uncertain legs unable to walk even a step. The calf struggled to hold its head up, not unusual for a newborn. I paid no attention to the cow as I ran behind Lassie toward the newborn. Carolyn and Sandy hung back and studied the situation.

"There's something wrong with that cow," Carolyn cautioned. "She's pawing the ground with her hooves and now she's bellowing. She looks mad at us. Pat, don't go any closer. Let's get Clarence to help us. We'll get Daddy to help us. Something is wrong! Listen to Lassie's bark!" Carolyn's caution changed to sudden fear.

"Pat, don't take any chances! Come back!" Sandy yelled.

"We always bring the calves to the barn. This calf is no different. Lassie and I will send it on the way to the barn and the cow will follow. Just like always."

Lassie's earnest barking continued as we moved closer. Suddenly, I noticed the half-crazed cow. I had been totally focused on the little calf. The cow was pawing the ground with one front hoof and then another, butting her head in my direction, and now bellowing mercilessly. I froze.

"Pat, come back! Carolyn's right. The cow is coming toward you and Lassie. That cow is going to attack you!"

In an instant, I knew there was imminent danger as I glimpsed the cow rapidly approaching Lassie, a little ahead of me. The cow was furious!

"Run, Pat! Run!" shouted Sandy.

The cow was as deranged as a mad bull in an arena. Lassie came to a sudden stop and turned toward me. She deflected the cow's attention, stopped in front of me, and then deftly turned in another direction and ran at full speed toward the newborn. The cow pursued Lassie as I hurried to my sisters. Lassie suddenly swung around and ran toward the three of us at full speed. She reached us again and nearly nipped our heels so anxious was she to move us away from danger.

"Let's go!" we screamed and ran as fast as we could.

Lassie lagged behind, stood her ground, barked at the cow menacingly, dodged the cow's continued pursuit until the three of us were well on our way toward the barn. The rest of the herd was following its leader, with Lassie in the rear. The cow stopped bellowing, returned to her newborn, and began cleaning its body with her tongue.

We approached Dad and Clarence who were readying the milking machines.

"Whoa!" exclaimed Clarence. "You're all talking at once. Let's hear that again." Dad and Clarence were all ears.

Carolyn spoke for the three of us and told our tale.

Dad commanded, "Leave the cow and her young one for now. Go ahead, feed the cows and calves. Clarence will take the tractor and the trailer and get the calf after our milking is done."

My brother nodded and they both returned to work. After feeding the animals, we raced to the house with Lassie and repeated our story to Raymond, Harriet, and

Mom.

Raymond teased, "You're just 'fraidy cats. You're sissies. Who's afraid of a cow?"

"Well, you go get that calf yourself! Then we'll see who the sissy is around here!" Sandy was the feisty one.

"Well! Look who's being bossy!"

My father entered the house. "There's no need for sharp tongues over a newborn calf. Clarence is hitching the trailer to the tractor, and he needs a couple of helpers."

"I'm not going. I might get killed by a nasty cow. Who's afraid of an old cow?" Raymond laughed.

"I'll go. I'll help Clarence," offered Harriet.

"Me, too," chimed in Carolyn, Sandy and I almost simultaneously. The four of us headed for the door with Lassie.

I hesitated, took Lassie by her collar and turned to Raymond. "We should keep Lassie in the house. That cow wants to hurt her."

"And what will I do with a barking dog? Pat, who appointed you the boss?"

I started to respond but heard the tractor approaching. The four of us bolted out the door. Four sisters and Clarence, the giant among us, were about to experience one of the many dangers Dad had warned us about.

We hopped on to the trailer and sped away. I could hear Lassie's frenzied yelping from inside the house. At the gate to the pasture, I jumped down, opened it, and after passing through, closed the gate, and hopped back on the trailer.

Clarence sped up a bit. In the distance, we girls could see the Guernsey and her calf. Everything looked normal enough. No big deal. I thought that maybe Raymond was right after all. Maybe my sisters and I had exaggerated any possible danger.

As we approached the cow, we knew instantly that Lassie's instinct to protect us was not from our naive imaginations. The cow again began pawing the sod with one front hoof and then the other. She butted her head toward the tractor. She let out frenetic bellows. Luckily, I thought to myself, our cows have been dehorned.

The little calf, now a few hours old, was alert and curious. It began sniffing the air and peering intently at the tractor and trailer. The calf gazed at us quizzically and took a step or two closer. His ears perked up as Clarence turned off the tractor's motor.

Clarence climbed down from the tractor's seat, and walked the few feet to the calf expecting to coax it by leading it to the trailer. The cow charged at Clarence. She butted at the air with her head and held a position between him and the calf. Clarence quickly retraced the few feet he had taken and climbed back up on to the tractor's seat.

He studied the situation. "Harriet, I'll get off again and

get the cow's attention. You get off, pick up the calf, and put it on to the trailer. Carolyn and you little kids get ready to help."

We watched. Clarence jumped down, this time to serve as a decoy. The cow, as predicted, moved toward Clarence.

"Now! Harriet, get the calf now! Quick! Quick!"

Harriet stepped from the trailer to the ground. Suddenly everything was a fury of rapid motion. The cow swung away from Clarence and toward Harriet and bellowed. The cow's head butted Harriet sending her sprawling to the ground. The Guernsey began stomping and clawing at my sister's body with furious hooves. Blood sprayed from Harriet's scalp. Her legs, bruised and red, were swelling fast. Her shirt was torn, her back scraped, and bleeding from the clawing hooves.

Clarence grabbed the pitchfork, carelessly left on the trailer, and charged the cow. When the cow felt the pain of the tines in its flanks, she swung around toward Clarence. Clarence struck the animal in the nostrils with the tines, stunning the cow.

All the while Clarence yelled, "Harriet, get up! Harriet, get up!"

The three of us from the trailer yelled, "Harriet, get up! Harriet, get up!" repeatedly. Harriet lay still, motionless, the back of her scalp red with oozing blood and her hair soaked red.

Clarence smartly raced around the tractor and leaped back on to its seat. The cow, now recovered, rounded the tractor in pursuit of Clarence. Harriet, for the moment, was free of the cow's torturous blows.

We girls continued to shout, "Harriet, get up!" Finally, Harriet managed to rise up on one shaky knee, then the other, and brought herself to a hunched position. She staggered on wobbly legs to the trailer. Carolyn grabbed one of her arms and helped her climb up. Harriet collapsed on to its wooden floor. Sandy and I stared at her in shock. Clarence started up the tractor, and at full throttle sped away, tires spinning in the grass.

"Stop screaming! Sandy! Pat! Stop that screaming!" Clarence's deep voice could be heard clearly, in spite of the roaring tractor.

Harriet, her scalp bleeding and red bruises on her legs and back, lay quiet on the trailer as we bumped over the rough pasture. Blood dribbled from strands of her hair on to her torn shirt and trickled forming little red pools on the trailer's floor. As we sped along, her torn shirt rippled in the breeze, exposing her injured back.

Sandy cried uncontrollably. She and I, teeth clenched, grasped each other's hands. Carolyn stroked one of Harriet's arms and murmured, "You'll be okay, Harriet. You'll be all right. We're almost home."

You can imagine the confusion when we entered the kitchen. Everyone spoke at once. Lassie yipped at her place beside the stove.

Sandy, the swiftest among us shouted, "Mom! Dad! Harriet's hurt! Hurry! Hurry! Daddy, she's bleeding!"

My mother rushed outside with Raymond. Lassie and Dad hurried close behind.

Mother took one look at Harriet who was struggling to stand. "We're going to the hospital. You help Harriet into the car, Raymond."

Raymond, staring at his sister, froze.

Mom demanded, "I mean right now! And, Dad, call the hospital. Tell them we're coming! She has a head injury. Tell them that."

"Come Harriet, lean on me. I'll help you," Raymond finally stammered as he and Carolyn helped Harriet to the car.

Inside the house, we told Dad what had happened. He said little, a sign of pensive thought. Lassie lay whimpering on the floor. I sat on the floor comforting her.

***

Later after Harriet had recovered, Mom praised Raymond for his help on that day.

"You reassured your sister during that drive to Randolph. Getting there seemed to take forever. I've forgotten what you two talked about. But I heard your voices. Harriet's was so weak."

"Well, I had read about a nurse's life during some war or other. She rescued wounded soldiers and she talked or sang to keep them awake until a medic was available. I decided that Harriet needed to stay awake."

"What did you talk about?" asked Carolyn.

"I asked Harriet simple questions like her name, her age, her address, her friends' names, her teacher's name, things like that. Mom was going so fast I worried we might not make it."

"You also asked me for my secret ingredient for my apple pies," beamed Harriet. "You helped me forget my troubles for a few minutes."

"You told him your secret ingredient?" I was dumbfounded.

"Yes, but I made it up."

Raymond laughed, "I knew Harriet would be okay if she could keep her secret during such a stressful time. And, you didn't fool me for I knew that dill pickle juice couldn't be a secret ingredient for a sweet apple pie. I was thinking that maybe I'd be a rescue agent, a medic, or something like that as we rode along."

"Son, you're coming into your own. You're full of surprises," Dad said.

At the hospital, Dr. Woodruff had shaved off a large patch of Harriet's hair. Her scalp was sewn together with several stitches. She had worn a bandage that looked like a beanie cap. The doctor prescribed a special prescription for her pain. He gave Mother a bottle of iodine to saturate Harriet's wounds.

"Luckily, Harriet has no injured bones. Put fresh bandages on her wounds every day after you clean them. This will prevent your daughter from getting an infection. Use clean cotton swabs every day," Dr. Woodruff instructed.

Ray joked with Harriet, "With that skull cap you can go to synagogue with Gene Shapiro and his parents."

"It's summer but make sure she's warm. Wake her every two hours for a few days to prevent her from going into shock. She has had a severe trauma. Harriet is lucky to be alive or not more seriously injured." Dr. Woodruff continued, "Her legs are badly bruised. They will heal. The hoof wounds on her back are not serious, but use the iodine solution to keep them clean. Call me if she seems unaware of where she is. Harriet is young. She'll heal quickly. Be sure that she eats properly and has plenty of fluids. She must stay out of the barn until her wounds are healed. Here is a prescription for her pain."

Mother added, "The doctor said Raymond and all of us have been shocked by this tragedy."

"Harriet is so lucky not to have to go to that wretched old barn," said Raymond.

"Let's see how lucky you'd feel after a cow beats you up!" Sandy was not afraid to tell Raymond details of her feelings. "Clarence and Carolyn were heroes, too. They saved Harriet from getting killed by that cow," Sandy began to cry.

"Carolyn helped her up onto the trailer and talked with her when we rode back to the house," I added. "Sandy and I were too scared to do anything."

"You both screamed plenty loud!" Clarence laughed.

Lassie became Harriet's dog for a few days. Instead of sleeping on the floor in the bedroom Carolyn and I shared, Lassie lay at night on the floor in Harriet and Sandy's room. When Harriet could walk alone, Lassie followed her around the house. She whimpered and rested her head on Harriet's lap. "You'll be okay. I'm right here beside you. Now, drink your water and eat some food," she seemed to be saying.

I began to believe that Lassie was a special dog, more than just a good dog. She had done her best to warn us. She comforted my sister when she most needed it.

That evening as darkness approached, Clarence and Uncle Jim trekked to the pasture and retrieved both the cow and calf without incident. How, I never asked. No one did. The pitchfork, thrown to the ground during the chaos, was retrieved.

Clarence said to Uncle Jim, "I don't know who left that pitchfork on the trailer. I nearly moved it back to its hook before I left with the girls to get the calf."

"It was a good thing the pitchfork was there, wasn't it? It's a miracle the pitchfork was on that trailer."

"Yes, it was. I was doing everything I could and needed

help," Clarence said.

Because the calf, fawn colored with some white here and there and with liquid brown eyes was male, he fed on his mother's milk for two or three weeks. He then was sold to the local cattle dealer. Mr. Shapiro drove to our farm in his big truck one morning. He retrieved a rope halter and hurried into the barn. Soon he returned with the calf. I watched as he led the frightened calf up the truck's ramp.

"Hello there, missy. You can see that I have nearly a full truck today. These calves will provide good veal for the table."

The little calves were tied inside the truck by a rope with just enough slack to lie down on the straw-covered floorboard. Holstein calves, small Jerseys, and now a Guernsey, all males, filled the truck. I said nothing as bewildered-eyed calves peered out of the truck into the light. I walked away.

I had read that animals never forget. This cow butted the air with her head and pawed at the ground with her hooves whenever she saw Harriet. Lassie got the same from the cow and she, too, shied away from that cow with no name.

Raymond nagged Dad, "Get rid of that Guernsey. She's dangerous. Can't you see that she hates Harriet? She hates Lassie, too!" We all silently wondered why our father kept the mad Guernsey.

Many months later, I asked Harriet about the accident. She explained, "For the first time I learned the meaning of prayer. I guess I had prayed at church, but on that day I knew I was praying. I asked for help because I couldn't move. I don't remember the struggle to the trailer. I do remember hearing the words, 'Harriet, get up!' several times. It seemed that someone was helping me, lifting me, giving me courage and strength. The sounds seemed so far away. But my prayers were answered. Of that, I'm sure."

She continued, "In my dreams, I remember the bellows of that cow and her hot breath as she attacked. Her hooves kept hitting me. It hurt and I felt like I was being rolled around and around and around."

After the tragedy, we were more careful around our animals. The experience showed us what could happen, in just an instant. Among ourselves we asked, "What if the pitchfork had not been left carelessly on the trailer? What if, upon the discovery of the newborn calf, we had not heeded Lassie's warning yelps? What if the cow had succeeded in attacking Clarence? What if Lassie had followed the trailer?"

Whatever we thought, we kept mostly to ourselves. But, I often wondered why the Guernsey reacted as she did. She had calved before with no incidents. And I wondered why we had never given that cow a name. She calved again and again without causing any more trouble.

Chapter 11

PESKY PLANTS

Sweet childish days, that were as long
as twenty days are now.
William Wordsworth

"It's time to get started on the raspberries. They're ripening fast," Dad said one day in late July.

A large, uncultivated raspberry patch grew on our farm. It was time to get busy plucking the juicy fruit from their vines. And that is what we sisters and sometimes Raymond did. We endured the sweltering hot sun as it rose high in the sky on a simmering summer day.

We suffered through more problems than the burning sun. Around a raspberry patch, there are several obstacles. One is the raspberry vine itself because it has thorns similar to those on rose bushes. Together, we'd make the best of it. If I met up with a sharp thorn, I screamed, "Ouch! I've been attacked! Somebody get me out of here!"

Sandy kidded, "Quick! Call a doctor! Quick! Those raspberry thorns have attacked Patty!"

Sandy was more wary of another plant. "I hate burdocks! I don't care how pretty the blossoms are, Pat. They're worse than a bee's sting!"

When in blossom, a burdock is pretty, a soft delicate lavender. But don't be fooled! If anyone brushed against one, it became her best friend or worst enemy depending on how you view it.

At maturity, burdocks grow to a height of four feet and some higher than I was tall. They grow along the field around the raspberry patch and create a home for themselves along the roadsides, in the pastures, and near the barnyard.

As the burdock blossom turns brown and dries at the end of the summer, it becomes dangerous. The dry burdock has sharp points and can stick to anything: clothing, hair, or a dog's tail. The burdock won't let go!

When a burdock got caught in my hair, I could not pull it out. Instead, Harriet or Carolyn said, "I'll cut your hair. I'll get the scissors from Mom."

Raymond teased, "Pat, you look weird with that hairless patch on your head." And when Sandy was attacked, Ray might say, "Who cut your hair? Did Mrs. Cutting lose her senses when she cut it last week?"

Burdocks let loose in the winter and roll around on the snow. They are as light and airy as feathers when caught by a swift breeze. When my sisters and I maneuvered down our sloping hilly meadows on our sleds, we were careful not to meet up with deadly, loose burdocks. They travel with the wind, but seem to have their own power to go right after a woolen snowsuit, hat, scarf, or

Pesky burdocks any time of the year

mittens. Sometimes one burdock bumps into another, grasps each other's sharp tentacles, and becomes more deadly as five, six, seven, or more join forces and form a baseball-sized ball.

Lassie was terrorized by the burdocks, too. In the winter, the marble-shaped burdocks directed their attention toward Lassie's fur as she raced playfully through the snow to keep up with our speeding sleds.

"Come, Lassie, I'll cut away that patch of burdocks on your fur." Lassie lay quietly, but nervously, as Harriet removed the burdock ball.

When spring came around, the old burdocks showed their real purpose, for inside, were seeds, which gave way to find a good place to grow into new green plants. Another generation of pests had begun.

Dad had said, "They're hardy enough to take root just about anywhere."

Another obstacle to picking the raspberries was thistles. Thistles have deep pink blossoms. Oh! So pretty! But beware. Thistles grow thorns on their blossoms that like to pierce into fingers just like the burdocks.

"Thistles belong in a desert!" Dad said.

The fourth of the plants to worry about are nettles. They made my skin itch! itch! itch! If I rubbed up against them, I was in for trouble. Nettles grow on fuzzy-looking stems which are a mass of tiny needles that pierce into skin, make a home there, and cause red welts. Later, as they mature, nettles become u-shaped demons that stick to whatever they strike.

Lassie got into nettles, too. When I'd pet her, "Ouch!" Her fur became a miniature spear arsenal!

If anybody tells you that you are nettlesome, that is not a compliment. It means that you are a troublemaker and nobody wants trouble.

"Trouble only leads to more trouble," Dad told us many times. "Now don't be nettlesome!"

Nettles are not complementary either. As far as I know they do not go well with anything, except, perhaps the devil. However, when the plant is young, cottontail rabbits like to nibble the little seedlings.

Once inside the raspberry patch, we picked as many raspberries as possible. Over the years, as we walked around and reached for every ripe berry, paths formed and meandered through the patch.

One hot summer day as we worked in the patch, Mr. Langevin stopped to see Dad and to check on his bee-hives. Just as his big truck rumbled up and sputtered to a stop, a little cottontail rabbit sped away.

Mr. Langevin paused to greet us, "Bonjour and good day." He tipped his old, black hat and grinned.

He held one raspberry he had just plucked. "*La framboise*," he said, "French for your raspberry."

We giggled because when he said *la framboise* it sounded as if he said farm boy. Later on we teased Raymond. "Hey, there farm boy, where's your straw hat? Hey, farm boy where are your boots? "

Raymond retaliated by creating monster faces. "I'm no farmer and you can take that to the bank!"

Many creatures occupied the raspberry patch in or near it at berry-picking time. Bees darted from blossom to blossom, looking for berry blossoms or perhaps brown-eyed Susans, buttercups, white daisies, or morning glories. The bees stung anyone unlucky enough to be in their flight path.

Garter snakes slithered through the underbrush. I knew they were harmless, but that didn't seem to matter when I saw one glide by a foot or two away from my shoe. "Yeow!"

Carolyn was particularly bothered by snakes. "I hate

snakes! I despise them! I don't care if they're harmless," she declared after one startled her. Her day in the raspberry patch had ended.

Little songbirds twittered around on the lookout for the best raspberries to eat. Barn swallows dove and swooped for mosquitoes, flies, gnats, and other flying insects. They built their mud and straw nests in the barn's eaves from plenty of mud around the cows' watering tub and from straw found here and there.

After the swallows' eggs had been laid and newly hatched, the adult swallows swooped at the cows as they entered and left the barn. The cows seemed oblivious to their presence. The birds swooped, looped around, and dove at people, too. The swallows were protecting their young.

Dad cautioned, "Leave the swallows to themselves. They eat mosquitoes and other bothersome insects. Let them be."

Flies, gnats, and mosquitoes buzzed around my head. There were butterflies of all kinds. Beautiful orange and black monarchs, the large yellow swallowtails, and pale green cabbage leaf butterflies all found reasons to be near the raspberry patch. Various moths, too, flittered from blossom to blossom.

"All of these butterflies do the same work that bees do," I said to Sandy.

"What's that?"

"Mrs. Abbott told us in science class. Their wings and other body parts pick up pollen to take from plant to plant."

"How do you remember everything, Patty? I forget a lot of stuff they say at school."

"Dad says we need to listen better than we do most of the time."

"Hey, Pat look, a dragonfly! Do they do the same thing?"

"Yeah, I guess so."

When all the raspberries had been picked and our pails were full, we hurried to the house with our ample supply. We kids sorted our raspberries, tossing out the occasional too-ripe berry, leaf, or twig that had fallen into our pails.

"Thanks for the Kool-Aid, Raymee!" said Sandy as we enjoyed the ice-cold sweetness while we sorted.

"I made it just for you, kiddo!"

Mom mixed raspberries with sugar and pectin to produce raspberry jam. The mixture brewed in a large kettle on the stove creating a delightful aroma throughout the house. Cooked and cooled, the jam was stored in jars. Hot wax covered the jam. Even though lids were tightened on the jar, a layer of wax ensured the jam's purity. Carolyn created labels that read "Raspberry Jam, 1954."

"Hey, Carolyn, can you draw a raspberry on each

label? Miss Langevin draws a little red clover on her honey jar labels," Sandy asked.

"Maybe next time, I will."

We carried the filled jars to our basement's pantry. Harriet, our organizer, checked to make sure the jars were lined up properly on the shelves.

Throughout the winter, the jam sweetened our toast. Among my favorite foods were raspberry jam and peanut butter sandwiches. Sandy thought that jam tasted best on ice cream. And it was a real treat on a waffle or a pancake with Vermont maple syrup.

Raymond would select two quarts of the best fresh raspberries and place them in a bowl. He'd grab the rolling pin and measuring cups in the drawer, another large bowl from the cupboard, lard from the fridge, flour from its bin, and a wooden spoon from the utensil drawer. He reached for the heavy marble slab used to roll out pie dough.

"Jeeze, this is heavy!" he'd exaggerate. "I can barely lift this." Raymond was preparing raspberry pies!

At supper that day, Clarence said, "Today, I started cutting the hay. Tomorrow I'll rake it. Can you kids help with the haying for the next day or two?"

Chapter 12

THE HAYMOW'S SECRETS

It's big out there. But on the whole the world's a wonderful place.
E. B. White

My siblings and I stacked hay bales just right, one on top of another as they tumbled from the baler. Out in the hayfield, the tractor with Clarence at the wheel pulled the hay baler. Behind the baler, the wagon moved all three machines in tandem. My siblings and I took turns and lifted a bale as each dropped from the baler onto the wagon. We steadied ourselves as the wagon slowly lurched across the bumpy field.

Then the wagonload was brought to our barn. There the bales were restacked in the haymows. Nice even rows were our specialty. My siblings and I were proud of our work. It was one task that was easily visible when completed. Hundreds of hay bales were stacked and ready for the cows to eat when the cold winter came. Finally, after many trips to the barn's haymow, the baling was complete. Haying takes up many weeks of a summer vacation.

Clarence had mowed the hay two days before. The mower, with the aid of the tractor, cut the hay within an inch or two of the ground. A day or two later, he had raked the hay into neat, mounded rows to dry its underside. He used the tractor this time to pull the rake.

Clarence had said, "Damp hay stored in a haymow causes the hay to molder or deteriorate. As it decays it loses its nutrients. And the cows dislike the taste of moldy hay."

You may have heard the expression, "Let's make hay while the sun shines." Anyone who lived on a farm listened to the radio for weather reports during the haying season. Dad read the weather reports in the paper. And our family forecast the weather. We watched for signs of oncoming thunderstorms. Billowy, white clouds could darken suddenly and fill the sky. Or a sudden breeze might come up and create a darkened sky as masses of moisture-filled air rolled in over the hills. We knew that rain was imminent.

"This morning, the sun was shining, and now it's raining pitch forks," mourned Clarence as he thought about having to re-rake the hay.

"Last week you said it rained cats and dogs," laughed Sandy. "Make up your mind, Clarence."

It was in the haymow that our barn cats created a home for their newborn. I loved the fluffy, furry kittens so soft and velvet-like. I accepted the challenge of taming the kittens with a bowl of warm milk. I brought a filled bowl and set it near, but not too close, to them.

The kittens hissed and held up their little tails just

Bailing and stacking hay in Vermont

like Mom cat to frighten away any oncoming danger. They never looked as dangerous as the mother cat, but they were learning fast.

"Here, kitty. Here, kitty," I called softly and coaxed them nearer to the bowl. They would inch right up to the milk if I had moved far enough away. "Here, kitty. Here, kitty!" With a watchful eye on me, they licked the milk with busy little tongues. To get a better advantage one or two stepped right into the bowl. They paused often to clean the sweet milk from their tiny paws.

It never took long for the kittens to lose their fear of me. When they spied me with that bowl, they bounded up, meowed, and pushed against my pant legs in anticipation of that magic milk supply. They soon learned to purr.

One at a time, I'd gather up a kitten and hold it close to my cheek petting it. Tiny little claws sometimes dug into my hands or cheek for each wanted to scramble down for more milk. I tried my luck with another kitten. "Who wants to be petted today? Kitty, come here, kitty." Tenderly, I'd scoop up another.

I said to Sandy, "I'll show you new kittens, but you mustn't touch these kitties until their eyes open. The mothers are protective and will not keep a very young kitten that has the smell of humans on its fur. A cat misjudges the kitten as a human and might even kill it. She has the safety of the whole litter in mind."

"Oh," said Sandy. "I didn't know that. She's a mean one, that old mother cat."

Although Sandy adored the kittens, once they matured, she lost interest. But one time she said to me, "Do you know that cats can swim?"

"That can't be so," I argued. "Cats aren't water animals, so, they don't swim."

We discussed the matter. Sandy was determined and inventive. "I know how to prove I'm right. Let's put a cat in water. Let's put one in the cows' watering tub."

"Oh! The tub is too deep! What if the cat drowns?"

"It won't drown. You'll see. Come on, let me show you. What's wrong with you, Pat? Are you afraid I'm right? You sound just like Raymond."

"All right, I'll try it. But we can't use Jimmie."

Dad had bought a large, deep wooden tub about eight feet in diameter. There in our barnyard, at any time, a cow could get a cool drink of water. A water tap continuously flowed ensuring a fresh supply. The water flowed from our spring via a long underground pipeline. It kept our cans of milk cool in the milk-house cooler. Water overflowed from the cooler to the tub and caused no problem except muddy conditions around the tub.

"Okay, let's try it." I was doubtful.

Sandy's experiment began. She and I selected a nice grown, male cat but nobody's favorite. Sandy situated herself around one area of the tub and I positioned myself directly across from her. Holding the cat over the tub with both hands, I hesitated. Then timidly, I dropped the cat into the water. *Splat!*

"Let's see if you can swim," I stammered.

And there in three feet of water, the cat began its journey to the other side of the tub. Upon reaching the other side, Sandy turned, as a toy, the frightened but swimming cat around and he swam back to me. Terror filled his eyes as his front paws paddled furiously just below the water's surface.

When the frantic cat reached me, I grabbed and lifted him out of the water. Panicky by now, the cat dug his claws into my arm. "Ouch! My arm!" I dropped the cat safely to the ground.

The cat shook his body several times, ridding himself of the water that matted his fur. He took a step or two and kept an eye on us. He shook his body a final time and rushed off in search of safety. I whimpered at my scratched and bleeding arm.

"Oh, that cat dug its claws right into my arm. Look at that! I'm bleeding!"

Sandy showed no remorse. "I told you so! NOW, do you believe me?"

She was right. Cats can swim, not happily nor with agility, but they can swim. In water, they are a little like fish out of water.

Some kittens were striped, either gray or yellow. And others were totally black, black and white, tawny, or three colors: white, black, and orange. Most of them were the shorthaired tabby types. I loved every cat that came along.

Cats on a farm were very useful and more than worth the bowls of warm milk they consumed. You see, cats adored a farm's worse enemy. That enemy was small, covered with gray fur, grew a long tail, saw with two bright, beady little eyes, and moved on four legs that scooted around really fast. The mother of these creatures gave birth to fifty babies a year! They also lived in the haymow or close to it. The mother used hay and straw and built a little nest for their home. ... Yes, a little gray mouse!

A mouser

Mice knew where the grain bins and burlap bags of oats were stored. The grains were for the calves, cows, and pigs and luckily Dad had planted a field of oats. Grain was expensive and if the mice ate it, that was "a very big loss," Dad said more often than I can count. The cats were a tad faster than the mice when it came to being tricked and caught. Dad called the cats his mousers.

Over time, many litters of kittens were born in the haymows. After the teacher read the note I presented to her upon arrival for another day of school, she turned to the class and said, "Pat's mother wants you to know that she has some kittens to give away. See Pat at recess if you need another cat."

Other farm kids did the same. There was an ongoing

supply. The teacher was always reading some Mom's note about cats to give away.

Some cats disappeared. I knew Dad or Mom had taken them to *that place.* I didn't need to ask or even talk about it. Dad had begun by saying, "We have too many cats again, way too many cats. Something has to be done."

In resignation, I looked for more kittens in the hay-mow. Usually I found another cat with a litter. If their eyes were closed, I knew they were still babies. At nine days old, they peered out at the world into which they had been born. In a tipsy way, they tottered around, a few awkward steps at a time. When they spied me, they raised their tails as if a flag on a pole. Their backs arched, fierce hissing sounds spewed from their mouths, snarls, and growls too. They were preparing themselves to frighten away any wrongdoer.

Mom cat watched her kittens totter around very worried if they strayed too far. Sometimes instinct told her to move the litter to a new area. She found a suitable place, and one at a time, clutched a kitten's nape in her mouth, and moved them to a safer home. Looking around carefully, I usually found them again in another area of the haymow.

Kittens grow fast. In one week, a kitten doubles in size. And after three weeks a kitten is four times larger. At a month old it looks for other things to eat. The Mom cat catches mice for them to gnaw on because by now the kittens have developed good, strong teeth.

At ten weeks old a cat lives independently. As a kitten it had played, leapt, ran, pounced, and twisted. Those swift movements now allow the kitten to hunt its own food. Soon enough, a growing cat produces its own family. The kittens have grown into full-sized mousers!

My favorite cat was named Jimmie. He was as big as a Maine coon cat, an armful. Jimmie had been one of those little kittens. Right from the start, he was special. His purr was the loudest I ever heard. He was the hungriest and the fastest kitty I'd ever seen. And his fur! His fur was the longest and the softest of any kitten I'd ever held.

Jimmie grew to be enormous. My brothers, sisters, and I constantly marveled at his size. Even Raymond noticed. "That cat thinks he's a dog. Look how big he is. He acts like a dog the way he curls up with Lassie at night. He follows Lassie everywhere."

Jimmie and Lassie never grew tired of romping through the fields and pastures. They made themselves at home in our house. Jimmie was one of the few cats allowed in our house.

Raymond observed, "Your bedroom looks like the barn with all those animals in there. Mother, those animals should sleep in the shed at night."

My mother remained quiet and did not voice an opinion about Raymond's newest issue.

"It's none of your business! Just mind your own business!" Both Carolyn and I remarked pointedly to Raymond.

My dad explained, "Raymond, listen. The girls' bedrooms are of no concern to you. You're too persnickety!"

Our bedroom seemed normal to me. We each had a bed. Our room contained a throw rug and we shared a big bureau. A lamp was over each bed. Our window sported a lacy curtain and a sunshade. The window was screened, and when opened during the summer, fresh cool air rolled up into our room as the sun set far off on the horizon.

The evening sky sparkled with a show of bright, shiny stars. The moon in various phases was there for the viewing. Carolyn and I named the constellations. We shared the few facts about space we had learned at school. We had read in our science books that humans could never reach the moon because it was so far away.

"The full moon looks almost close enough to touch," Carolyn said. "Good night, Pat. Good night, Lassie. Good night, Jimmie."

"Good night, everybody," I replied. Lassie thumped her tail against the rug and Jimmie purred. I fell asleep.

Chapter 13

MONSTER MACHINERY

The older generations can remember when it was unthinkable to operate a Vermont farm without horses for work, for transportation and - yes! for companionship!
Harry H. Cooley

Carolyn sleepily asked, "Pat, what's the matter with you? Why are you crying? Are you sick or something?"

At the same moment, Mom rushed into the bedroom, and switched on the light. "Pat, what is wrong?"

Lassie awoke, startled by the sounds. Jimmie scampered off, his sleep disrupted.

"I don't know," I stammered. "I was having a bad dream."

Mom left the room. "The best thing to do is to go back to sleep. It's midnight. Get some sleep. Tomorrow is the Fourth of July. We need a good night's rest."

It was nearly time for the town parade, fireworks, a barbecue, and all kinds of excitement. On that hot night before the Fourth of July and after finally falling asleep, I was awakened by Carolyn and Mother. My dreams were of being gathered up by a huge, ugly monster. I scrambled in a futile attempt to get out of its approaching path. I could not sleep and my mind relived the event of the day. I lay awake tossing and turning in my bed.

***

By the time I was a toddler, Dad had modernized our farm with new machinery. Our two horses were no longer needed because tractors had replaced them. Machinery planted seeds. They cut, raked, baled the hay, and chopped the corn. Machines planted and would soon harvest our oats. Machines spread manure and fertilizers. Machines assisted in every aspect of the daily work on the farm and much tedious, hard labor had been eliminated. Our Farmall tractor was busy, busy, busy.

"The machines are busier than we are. A lot of back-breaking work is no longer necessary. Machines even milk our cows and spread their manure," Dad said.

Harriet told me about the days when Dad had owned a team of horses.

"The horses are no longer needed," Daddy told Harriet. "He said he didn't know what to do with them. So he decided to put Beauty and Lucky out to pasture. The horses were friendly. They ate apples out of my hand, liked to be petted, and stood still while I reached to brush their manes. Daddy put me up on Beauty's back and let me ride while he led her with a halter."

"Did Daddy name Beauty for Black Beauty, you know, the one in the book?" I asked.

"I don't know. Beauty was a male and Lucky was a female. One day Daddy told Mom that our horses had

Beauty poses with Chase children, mid 1940s

been put out to pasture. Their work was done. He said they deserved a rest until their time came. Daddy said he hoped that he would like his machines as much as he liked his horses."

"I have a foggy memory of the two slow horses, Beauty and Lucky, lumbering around the pasture. I remember seeing them drink water from the brook. They ate green grass in the pasture right along with our cows. And when it rained, they found shelter in the horse barn."

"I don't remember when their 'time had come.' But one day they were gone. They had been sold," Harriet said.

"I don't remember either."

Even though my family had learned to be careful around motorized machinery, we did not always practice caution. Yes, we had heard of disasters, such as a loose sleeve getting caught in a machine with tragic results of a mangled arm or worse. We had heard about farm injuries with hay balers. Someone run through a hay baler compressed the body just at it did the hay and caused severe injury, even death.

One of Harriet's friends was injured as she hid in tall hay her dad was cutting with a new mowing machine. Rita, a toddler at the time, planned to surprise her dad as he worked.

"Rita has only her thumb and parts of a couple fingers on one hand. The others were sliced off by the mowing machine. Her dad never saw her," Harriet said.

***

Now, Clarence was the operator of the machinery. We little kids knew that we should not be near any machinery unless we were helping Clarence or Dad. On that hot day in July, all of us kids were excited about the upcoming July 4th celebration. But something happened that caused my scary nightmare.

Clarence had cut the hay in one field, raked it, and now it was ready to bale. Most of the time, we attached the large wagon to the baler and stacked the bales on to the wagon as they sprang from the machine. This time was different because no one was around to help except me. And one little kid wasn't enough help to stack the bales.

Where was everyone? Mom and Raymond were in the kitchen cooking up a storm. Dad had driven the car to buy eggs at Mr. Adams poultry farm. I had been riding my bike along the country roads surrounding our farm. When I returned home, I discovered that my sisters had

Raked hay ready for baling in Randolph Center

gone with my father. I was angry because I had missed the fun of going to Mr. Adams's poultry farm with Dad and my sisters.

Clarence said, "I'm going to bale the hay anyway. Tomorrow is the Fourth of July. I want to get it done so we can go to the parade and you kids can go swimming. We'll go to the barbecue. Later today, we'll gather the bales with the wagon. Want to come along, Pat?"

"Oh, sure," I said with budding enthusiasm.

And so, Clarence and I headed for the neatly raked rows of hay. I stood on the narrow hitch that attached the baler to the tractor and held on to my brother's shoulders to steady myself. From my perch, I could see everything in front of me. As we passed the forested area, I watched black crows flying overhead. "Caw, Caw," they crowed as they darted from tree to tree. The tractor's motor and rumbling baler frightened a little rabbit into a nearby bush. The sun shone brightly through a cloudless, blue sky.

"Darn," I said to myself, "I've forgotten my hat."

In the field, Clarence positioned the baler so that it scooped up the narrow rows of hay as he slowly moved along. Then it was compressed as hay traveled through the baler. The bales were automatically tied with twine just before each fell out on to the ground.

The sun became hotter and hotter as high noon approached. Bees buzzed around looking for wildflowers. The tractor and baler noisily moved along and scooped up row after row. A cloud of dust roiled up from the nearby road as a truck or car occasionally sped by.

I felt the warmth from the sun. My arms were warm and the top of my head was feeling hotter by the second. I squinted into the midday sky. The sounds of the tractor and the baler grew monotonous. I felt drowsy, sleepy, then sleepier ... and sleepier.... And just like that, I felt myself hit the ground right in the path of the oncoming baler! I was stunned by the prickly feeling on my legs, arms, and face as they met the stubble of mown hay. I crawled as fast as I could out of the way of the approaching machine, but its tire rolled over my left shoe. I screamed! I screamed again and again.

Clarence looked back and saw me there in the field, braked the machine and hopped off. I saw him push his baseball cap up for a better view. "What happened to you?"

"I just fell off." I was shaking and trying to stand.

"Are you okay?" He reached and pulled me to my feet.

"I think so. The tire ran over my foot, but it's all right I guess." I walked a few wobbly feet, stepping gingerly on my left foot. I winced with pain. "It's okay."

"Lucky you, you're wearing your work shoes. That's a close call. You could have been scooped up by the hay baler. Don't tell anybody. I know you're not supposed to ride on the hitch. What happened to you anyway?"

"I just fell off.... I don't remember how."

I walked to the house and Clarence continued his work. I wasn't hurt, just a little pain in my left foot and a few scratches on my arms, face, and legs from the stubble. Inside my head though, I felt rattled and shaky.

"What if?" I wondered as I made my way to the kitchen, greeted Ray and Mom, drank a glass of cool water, and went outside with Lassie.

I sprawled on the lawn in the shade of the maples, Lassie by my side. I slid off my shoe and sock. I was shocked by the color of my foot! No big deal, but, how could I go swimming on the Fourth of July with my foot covered with black and blue splotches? I quickly replaced my shoe and sock.

Finally, Dad and my sisters returned and Sandy ran over to see me. "What have you been doing, Patty? Mr. Adams showed us how eggs are graded with his new machine. He turns a switch, the eggs roll out, and they're automatically weighed."

"Oh, I just got off my bike. I've been sitting here with Lassie waiting for you," I lied. "How many eggs did Dad buy?"

"He bought extra eggs because Raymond is making something special. The new egg machine is automatic. The little ones go in one direction and the big ones in another."

"Oh, will we still have a watermelon tomorrow? I love watermelon. And you do, too."

"I think so. But Raymond found a special recipe used by Mrs. Lincoln to celebrate her husband's winning the election almost a hundred years ago. He wants to try it. The recipe takes lots of eggs."

"What does the Fourth of July have to do with Abraham Lincoln's election? Just as long as we can have watermelon, I'll be happy. What's he going to make?"

I stood up and headed toward the house with Sandy. My foot was sore and I winced and limped a little.

"It's some kind of cake. Where's Clarence? Hey, is something wrong with your foot? Why are you limping? Did you scratch your arm? It's all red spots. Hey, your leg is too!"

"Clarence is baling hay all by himself. No, nothing's wrong with my foot or leg, and nothing's wrong with my arm either. He said we'll pick up the bales later."

How could I swim if my foot was black and blue? What if it continued to swell? What if I was unable to stand during the parade? Would I be able to stand in the long line for the Coca-Cola and all the food at the barbecue?

Raymond noticed everything. What if Raymond noticed my foot...or my scratched arm...or my limp? I asked myself over and over. Fears rolled around in my head. I had no answers to allay them.

"I'll never ride on the tractor hitch again," I promised myself.

I heard Lassie settle down on the carpet and the occasional thumping of her tail. Jimmie returned and cuddled up in his place near Lassie. I finally drifted off to sleep.

Clarence and I kept the secret about that near disaster. To my knowledge, he never told anyone about our escape from a near-tragedy, but we both learned a valuable lesson that day.

Chapter 14

MENDING FENCES

My apple trees will never get across
And eat the cones under his pines, I tell him.
He only says, "Good fences make good neighbors."
Robert Frost

Sandy and I had watched the parade. We cheered all of the high school kids, including Raymond, who were marching in the high school band. He played his trumpet as he marched through town with the rest of the band. The band played lively Sousa marches. The town fire truck volunteers tossed lollipops to all the kids.

"Hurry up, Pat! We can get a lot if we hurry. Come on!" Sandy impatiently demanded.

True to his word, Raymond filled our plates generously as we passed through the long lines at the Rotary Club's barbecue. As we feasted on coleslaw and chicken, we sat at long tables and enjoyed the sounds all around: people laughing and talking, the splashes of swimmers as they dove off the diving board into the river, and the calls of the clown who greeted everyone and wanted to shake their hands. Some Rotary Club members handed out little flags.

When the day ended, life soon enough returned to our daily routine. Dad said, "Farming is one thing after another." And the Fourth of July had come and gone.

Keeping the heifers within their fenced-in pasture was very important. Heifers were our young cattle and enjoyed staying outdoors all summer. They lived in the far-off pasture and ate the grasses and drank water from the brook. Every spring, Dad checked the fencing for weak links. "No heifer will break through the fencing this year. I've checked every barbed wire and fence post. The fencing is as strong as a fort."

"I think the heifers are looking for some fun," Sandy said after they had managed to break through their fence.

"Why?" I asked.

"Dad says they're the teenagers and before they grow up, they act foolish."

Imagine the damage a few heifers can do to a garden or to someone's tidy lawn. Once in a while a few of them, and sometimes the cows, managed to break through their fence. Most likely a fence post had broken and loosened the barbed wire that connected the posts to each other. With that broken link, the animals owned a pass to temporary freedom.

Whenever the animals got loose Dad explained, "They think the grass is greener on the other side of the fence."

I knew how to mend fences, real fences. I also knew about the kind of fence mending required when you solve a serious problem. Sometimes a neighbor called to report that our animals were out. When someone reported that, we hopped to the rescue. Pronto!

The heifers were apt to be eating vegetables in a neighbor's garden, the grass on the family lawn, or the young cornstalks in a cornfield. The cattle destroyed young plants with heavy hooves. My siblings and I gathered up a hammer and a few u-shaped nails and headed off to chase them back into their proper place, the pasture. Before returning home we'd struggle to repair the fence's broken place.

In this case, Mrs. Farnsworth had already chased the animals from her lawn and garden. They seemed to be waiting aimlessly for us when we arrived. Mrs. Farnsworth stood at her opened front door and greeted us.

"I'm glad you're here. Your animals have messed up the garden and the lawn. They've been running around all over my yard. Ask your father to call me right away."

"Yes, Mrs. Farnsworth, we'll ask Dad to call you when we get back to our house," Carolyn spoke for all of us.

The heifers were easy to chase back into the pasture. They knew where they belonged. They marched right back through the break in the fence. They aren't dumb.

As best we could, we kids repaired and re-attached the barbed wires to the cedar posts. Sometimes the fence posts were too old, too weathered, or too broken to use.

An old barbed wire fence in need of repair

Their only use now was for fuel at the sugarhouse. When the repair was completed, we trudged back home.

"They think the grass is greener on the other side of the fence. What does that mean anyway, Patty?" Sandy giggled as she repeated the phrase often used by Dad.

"That means you need to look at what you have. Dad thinks we have everything we need. So if you want something, it's right where you are," I explained.

"Oh, okay, Daddy says you can't have everything right now at this minute. Does that mean the same thing?"

"Yeah, I think so."

Whenever Dad gave advice, Raymond rolled his eyes, shrugged his shoulders, and imitated him. With exaggerated hand and facial signals, he'd copy Dad's mannerisms and then begin his speech with a firm voice.

Mimicking Dad, he'd say, "Let sleeping dogs lie. The grass is greener on the other side of the fence. A stitch in time saves nine, just as if he were a poet or something. Honestly I'm sick of his preaching."

We laughed with Raymond for he was part actor, part comic, with a dry sense of humor. He was very dramatic, and if you heard him for the first time, you might think he was completely serious. We knew he was kidding around. Dad knew also. Raymond got into trouble once in a while at school with his humor.

"You know, I said to Mrs. Perry, I was only joking around. I thought you'd laugh and not get angry." That day Ray avoided a detention and a trip to the principal's office.

Just like now, cedar was an excellent wood to use as fence posts and shingles because it was water resistant. Cedar was used by the pioneers for the same purposes. Because of its fine quality, the settlers used it for buckets, roofing, and other needs. Eventually, like everything else, the cedar posts wore out.

Our barn was not painted red like the kind you see in photographs and magazines. Instead it was built using cedar shingles. They were natural wood and weather worn.

"Having sensible, cedar shingles is one less thing to worry about. Shingles need no paint and will last un-

Deer can leap over fences and destroy crops

til time wears them out. They'll endure long after I am gone." Dad was a practical man.

When we returned home, Dad was enjoying a coffee break with Uncle Jim, our postman. Mom had informed our dad about the heifers, where we kids had gone, and he was waiting for us to return. We reported details of the animals' misdeeds.

"They were in the garden and on Mrs. Farnsworth's lawn. She wants you to call her right away," Carolyn said.

"They were eating the corn plants and one of them pooped on her lawn. I think Mrs. Farnsworth is really mad about that," Sandy added.

"We fixed the fence, but I think they can break through there again. Two fence posts broke in half and they walked right through," I explained.

Immediately, Dad got up from his chair, excused himself from the table, and said to Uncle Jim, "I've got to take care of this! Those heifers have all the grass and water they need. Why do they have to break through all the time?"

He nodded at us and headed for the phone. He picked it up from its cradle and quickly dialed Mrs. Farnsworth. He greeted her and asked, "Can you use some maple syrup? ... Yes, well, I will repair the fence right away." Or maybe, "Do you need some potatoes? ... Okay, of course, right away, yes."

Dad placed the phone in its cradle and said his good-byes to Uncle Jim. On his way to the door he messed up Sandy's hair.

"Thanks, Mary. I must get back on my route." Uncle Jim left to continue his mail delivery.

Following this conversation, Dad drove the truck to Mrs. Farnsworth's house. The truck carried a shovel, a hammer, a couple of new cedar posts, and a sledge-hammer. In his pocket, he carried a supply of u-shaped nails. He also took a gallon of maple syrup. He was mending fences in a couple of ways. Good fences make good neighbors; good relationships with your neighbors make good sense. That's something else my father believed. Dad practiced what he preached.

Chapter 15

THE GARDEN HARVEST

Come, ye thankful people, come,
Raise the song of harvest-home;
All is safely gathered in,
Ere the winter storms begin.
Henry Alfred

"Our basket is full to the brim!" called out Sandy as she and I harvested tender, green leaf lettuce, radishes, beet greens, and green tail onions. "I can't wait to have a lettuce and mayonnaise sandwich for lunch."

Throughout the summer our family harvested vegetables from the garden. We ate fresh vegetables with every meal during the harvesting season.

Within a few days, Sandy exclaimed, "Look at the peas! They are about to burst from their pods. And the cucumbers are getting bigger."

My sisters and I picked each pea pod exploding with six or seven peas inside. Our baskets were full, and we carried them to our front porch. There in the shade of our maples, we shelled the peas by removing each pea from its pod. Soon our large wooden bowls were filled with pebble-sized green peas.

On our farm, we wasted nothing and that was true for the pea pods. What good are empty pea pods? Our pigs loved them and scampered up to their long, narrow trough with coiled tails that wiggled like a whirligig.

"Oink! Oink!" they'd grunt as they looked up at us with bright little eyes. It was difficult to decide whether they were hungry or happy. Perhaps they were both. Regardless, they loved the pea pods by the truckload. Just kidding!

We ate some of the peas right away. Other peas were frozen in our freezer for winter use. Still others were sold to Mrs. Hodgdon for use at her rooming house. She also bought premium potatoes and squash. My father delivered the produce to her in Northfield. While he was there, he stopped to see if Norwich University was ready for more potatoes or squash. He carried extras.

Dad and the rest of us loved peas mixed with cut-up pieces of potatoes. We consumed lots of potatoes. The round peas and dice-shaped potato cubes swam in a pool of warm milk with salt, pepper, and butter.

"Real butter! And not that stuff called margarine the grocers sell at the A&P grocery store. Trying to make lard look like butter is the most foolish thing I've heard of." In truth, Dad didn't like the competition of margarine. Many people chose to buy margarine, overlooking butter, because it was cheaper.

The green beans and wax beans were easily harvested. "Let's see who can fill their basket first: you and me or Harriet and Carolyn." Sandy made a game of it all.

Usually Harriet and Carolyn managed to fill their basket first. Of course, Sandy and I were the "little kids" and no one expected us to be first.

Our kitchen cutting board was put to use just as it had been for cutting the rhubarb. That miniature guillotine quickly cut the beans into bite-sized lengths. I stacked the beans into a few rows, some on top of each other. Then as I cut the beans I slid the rows along an inch or so. Stack, slide, cut! Stack, slide, cut! Stack, slide, cut! Just be careful not to cut off a finger.

"Hey! It's my turn to use the cutter!" Sandy grabbed some beans.

Mom put a small amount of water into the pressure cooker to pressure cook jars of green beans just as she had done with the tomatoes and the beets. Once cooked and cooled, my sisters and I carried the jars to the basement always careful that none dropped. The shelves in the pantry filled up.

Harriet said, "Put all the green beans on this shelf. Push them all the way back to the wall. We have a lot of green beans."

Later in the summer, we picked the dry beans: the great northern beans, the kidney beans, and the pole beans. They were drying in their pods and were now ready for harvest. The pole beans had grown high with the aid of the twine we had placed there earlier in the summer with Dad.

"Hey, I need a ladder to get way up there." Sandy exaggerated her reach.

"We need to get these beans picked. Look how brown the

pods are, and dry, too. If the pods burst, all the seeds will go to the chipmunks and squirrels," I said.

"Yeah, most are ready to pop out of the shells."

"That will make it easy to shell them."

"Look, Patty. Look how they pop right out!"

When harvested and shelled, the beans were laid out on cookie sheets and pans to completely dry. Soon the beans were piled high, and within a few days, they were placed in large crocks with lids on shelves in the freezer room. "Keep them in there," Mom said, "The basement is too damp for them."

"I like the beans baked with maple syrup and bacon." Sandy licked her lips.

"They're best when mixed up with some of our vegetables like carrots and potatoes. I heard Dad call it poor man's stew," I said.

"What? We're not poor! The kids down the road are poor. They don't have anything. We have a lot!" Raymond intervened. "We'll never be poor like that! Those kids look sick. Have you seen them walk by our house with their mother?"

"Yeah," both Sandy and I added.

"Save the bean pods in the old baskets. They're our flint and steel," Dad chuckled.

One of our kitchen stoves burned wood and the large, wood stove in our living room provided heat both upstairs and downstairs. Mom bought big wooden matches in cardboard boxes to kindle a fire with empty pods.

Two stoves sat in the kitchen, the wood-fired one and another electric one. Food was prepared on both stoves. The wood-burning stove was used in the winter for heat and for preparing stove-top type foods. It also contained an oven and Mom used it to bake bread twice a week. But the electric stove was used primarily for baking.

Dad called the electric stove "Raymond's Bakery" because when Raymond baked, the aroma of his baked goodies spread throughout the house. He preferred the electric stove because he could regulate the heat to a precise temperature. Raymond looked for perfection in everything he did.

"Mother, how do you know the temperature of the wood stove? How can you bake bread so perfectly without knowing the temperature?" asked Raymond scratching his head in wonder or perhaps bewilderment.

"With practice you'll figure it out. You'll get the knack of it." Mom smiled.

Another stove stood in the living room. During the winter, great chunks of wood fit into its firebox and radiated heat in all directions. Cast iron grates with smaller openings covered the holes in our ceiling and allowed warm air from our living room to travel up to the bedrooms to keep us warm during the winter.

Other vegetables such as beet greens, beets, Swiss chard, carrots, and spinach were harvested daily while the supply lasted. Some were preserved for winter use. A portion was consumed by our family right away. Of course, many vegetables were sold.

"Leave the parsnips in the ground until they are good and ready," my father said.

"Good and ready for what?" we kids asked.

Sandy answered, "Until somebody can stand the taste of them." Everyone laughed at Sandy's joke.

"I like parsnips the way you make them, Raymond. You cook them with carrots and butter and cut them up into little circles," I said.

"Thanks, kiddo. I make them just for you."

"And on a dinner plate, carrots and parsnips, yellow and orange, look pretty all cut into bite-sized pieces."

"You betcha, kiddo, I can make anything taste delicious, even woody, old parsnips!"

We picked the summer squash as soon as they were ready. The smaller they were the better they tasted. Whether boiled in water, fried with onions, or baked with cheese and potatoes, summer squash was a favorite.

Summer squash grew very fast as if by magic. One really big squash appeared and then another. And still another! My sisters and I gathered the too big ones, and Dad cut up the squash with a machete-sized knife.

We carried baskets full of squash to the pasture. Our Holsteins hurried over to see what we were doing. When cows are curious they can move fast. They chewed the squash with partially closed eyes, heads lifted skyward, and looked

Summer squash

very happy!

Cows belong to a group of mammals called ruminants and have compartments in their digestive system. Cows hurry and eat as much as they can. Later, they cough up a little food at a time and chew it. It's called a cud. The chewing goes on and on until "the cows come home," which means a long time of idle dreamy-eyed chewing.

We returned to the garden and gathered up more produce. Every day there were more vegetables to pick. Tomatoes seemed to be growing, ripening, and needing attention almost every day just like the beans, squash, beets, lettuce, and cucumbers. The carrots were getting larger and there were old wives' tales of dreaded happenings if we ate too many raw vegetables! On the danger list were two vegetables in particular: carrots and tomatoes!

Chapter 16

IDLE HANDS ARE THE DEVIL'S WORKSHOP

Nothing is really work unless you would rather be doing something else.
James Barrie

As my sisters and I harvested vegetables, we often snacked on our favorites. We brought new meaning to "fresh from the garden!" We pulled carrots from the earth and ate them raw. Tomatoes also traveled from plant, to hand, to mouth.

Aunt Almira, who often lived with us, thought that most vegetables needed to be cooked before they were eaten. "You children will get sick if your food is not cooked," she worried time after time.

In a well-rehearsed drama, Sandy and I chewed on a carrot, grabbed at our throats, and in one voice proclaimed, "Help! Help! These carrots are making us sick! They're full of poison! Help us! Call a doctor, be quick!"

Distraught, Aunt Almira warned us, "Tomatoes and carrots are poisonous until they are washed and cooked. Don't eat them yet!" She cried as we kids chewed on a carrot or sunk our teeth into a plump, juicy tomato fresh from its vine.

Dad explained why our aunt thought that way. "As a

Poisonous carrots...just kidding!

little girl, our Aunt Fannie told us that vegetables need to boil before we could safely eat them. Aunt Almira never learned differently. She has your best interest in mind when she says that."

"Have you heard about lead poisoning?" Dad asked. "Almira's fears are based on experiences of people when they placed cut-up uncooked tomatoes on pewter plates. Pewter contains lead and other metals. Tomatoes contain acid that causes lead to seep out of the pewter. When people became sick, they thought the uncooked tomatoes were the cause. Lead, released by the acid in the tomatoes, was the culprit."

Aunt Almira had other puzzling ideas. She was afraid of the dark. She was certain people were searching for her and wanted to harm her. When she stayed at her own house, she telephoned Dad late at night.

"There are noises in the carriage shed." Or, "I hear someone in the basement." Or, "I hear footsteps in the attic!" she would say to Dad after waking him.

"The last time I drove over, we decided the noise was from the wind blowing loose boards against the old shed." Or, "You know you have mice in your house. They must be running around. They'll soon go away because we set traps for them. Remember?" Dad spoke patiently to his sister.

"It's dark and I'm afraid. There are noises," she cried.

"Like I said, I'll drive right over as soon as the milking is done in the morning. You can make me breakfast. Okay?"

"I can't sleep."

"Do some crocheting or knitting. I'll check the mousetraps with you in the morning. Good night, now."

Aunt Almira suffered from emotional problems and spent time in a special hospital for treatment. When she was a little better, she lived with us. When she felt fine, she lived in her own house and sometimes worked.

"Be good to your Aunt Almira. She has had a hard life. She needs our help right now. She never knew her Daddy. She was a baby when he passed away," Dad reminded us. "I think that's why she has problems."

Aunt Almira crocheted doilies, washcloths, and dishcloths. She crafted delicate edges around pillow cases, napkins, and tablecloths. Her hands were always busy working on her projects or mending someone's socks, shirts, or pants.

"Idle hands are the devil's workshop," Aunt Almira would say as she worked with fast-moving hands.

"Your Aunt Almira learned how to crochet and knit when she was a child. Aunt Fannie taught her. That special hospital she stays at from time to time encourages her to keep busy. The nurses asked Almira to teach other patients how to crochet. And it's true, 'Idle hands are the devil's workshop'. You little kids should learn how to crochet," Dad told Sandy and me.

"Who else stays at that hospital?" asked Sandy.

"People who have mental problems stay there until they are well. Then they go back home or live with their relatives."

"Where is the hospital?" I asked.

"It's in Waterbury."

"Oh!" I was shocked. Sandy was, too. We looked at Dad.

Kids at school would fool around and say, "You belong in Waterbury. You're crazy!" Or, "You're so mental that you belong in the crazy house in Waterbury!"

Sandy and I said the same things to kids, too. "You're mental, sick in the head!" or "You've lost your mind! You belong in Waterbury."

"The Waterbury State Hospital helps your aunt get better. She has special treatments when she's there," Dad told us. "And our mommy passed away when she was five. Almira never got over losing her mother at so young an age and her daddy, too."

I began to think differently about people who were ill in that way. Sandy did, too.

Sandy and I tried to be good to Aunt Almira. However, sometimes we forgot and reacted to her ideas and puzzling behavior with foolish abandon. We ravaged her candy supply. We pulled her apron strings as she napped in her chair.

"Quick, go now!" I'd whisper to Sandy as she tiptoed toward our aunt. "Quick, untie her shoelaces!" Today I regret that childish behavior. Sandy, too.

We gathered up the turnips, beets, onions, and cabbages. Some were stored in the basement for later use. My mother cooked corned beef and cabbage until we were blue in the face. The beef was stored in brine in large crocks in the basement. The crocks had replaced large wooden barrels. Salt, spices, and water, or brine, preserved the corned beef. Cabbages also were stored in the brine. First, they had been washed and cut into wedges perhaps four or six to a cabbage. All winter long we ate corned beef and cabbage.

"I'm all cabbaged out!" I'd say at dinnertime.

"Me, too!" exclaimed Sandy. "When can we have some

other vegetable?"

Except for Raymond's coleslaw mixed with cut-up raw cabbage, carrots, and apples, I had had enough of that vegetable. Raymond added a handful or two of raisins to give extra flavor and sweetness to the coleslaw. His secret, however was mayonnaise mixed with sugar and vinegar.

"Ray, that's not much of a secret. That recipe is in our cookbook," Harriet teased.

My sisters and I gathered up green, leafy lettuce throughout the summer. We built sandwiches with the yeast bread Mom baked, and added lettuce, cucumbers, and sliced tomatoes slathered with mayonnaise.

We ate steamed spinach, Swiss chard, and big red beets. Overall, we had plenty of vegetables.

"Just like Popeye we have lots of spinach. I'm Popeye the sailor man. I'm Popeye the sailor man ..." Sandy happily sang and danced.

"Where are your muscles?" Raymond asked.

Sandy raised one small arm to demonstrate her powerful muscles. She gulped spinach by the forkful with her free hand and looked as wide-eyed as Popeye himself. Everyone laughed.

"If you're Popeye then you need a pipe clenched between your teeth," Raymond teased. "Maybe Santa will bring you tobacco and a pipe this year."

"You got a match?"

Harvested onions

My mother canned tomatoes and the biggest beets. As they cooked in the pressure cooker, we'd listen for the pop of the jar lids as they formed a vacuum against the jar rubber and the lids.

Some cucumbers became sweet pickles along with a few of our beets. They, too, were stored in jars in the pantry. We carried jar after jar of canned food into our basement.

The other part of the basement housed gigantic bins for our potato crop. Other bins were filled with our four types of squash. Still others held cabbages and onions. Carrots, in another storage bin, were covered with sand to be kept as fresh as possible.

Near the center of the basement sat the potato grader,

ready for use. A set of scales to weigh the potatoes was nearby, and off to one side lay piles of sacks and stacks of baskets used by our customers to carry away their purchases. Barrels of corned beef and cabbage in brine were in a far-off corner along with barrels of apples.

At the end of harvesting season, my father rubbed his tummy, messed up Sandy's hair, and chuckled, "Now we have enough food for the whole army."

Chapter 17

SACKS & SACKS OF OATS

Come, ye thankful people, come,
Raise the song of Harvest-home;
All is safely gathered in,
Ere the winter storms begin."
Henry Alford

One sunny morning, late in the summer, when all the hay was in the haymows and many of the garden vegetables had been frozen or canned, Dad picked up the phone and called Mr. Ferguson. "Our oats are ready for harvest. Can you get here this week with your harvester?"

"Okay, that's good. Thanks. Clarence and I will get our own sacks. We'll be ready for you on Wednesday." Dad set the phone in its cradle.

Dad had been frantic to stay ahead of the weather. Hard rains, thunderstorms, or strong winds could have destroyed his oat crop. Harvest time was here. He had watched the sky for thunderheads.

On Wednesday, my father's friend, Mr. Ferguson, arrived with his harvesting machine. He slowly towed the harvester to our field with his old truck. Mr. Ferguson complained, "I don't know why people in their cars are in such a hurry."

"Where are they going in such a rush? What's the hurry?

They go by our place like a house afire," Dad agreed with his friend's assessment of impatient drivers.

The oats, now amber in color, were ready for harvest. The seeds weighed just enough to cause the stalks to bend slightly without a breeze and to sway dance-like during any gentle breeze.

"Thank God there have been no strong winds or nasty thunderstorms. The oats are heavy and the stalks could break if the winds are too strong and severe. That would ruin our crop." Dad said time and again.

"How many times are you going to give us a weather report about the oats, Dad?" Clarence kidded.

Mr. Ferguson drove our tractor and pulled his harvester up and down the rows of oats. First, the harvester cut the oat stalks close to the ground and they instantly fell on to the harvester's conveyor belt. A harvester is also called a thresher because the stalks were threshed or shaken to remove the oat seeds.

During the shaking, the oats were set loose from the stalks and fell away and up through a tube into the back of the harvester. Two burlap sacks sat side by side and attached to the back of the machine. One at a time a sack was filled. The threshed stalks fell to the ground behind the conveyor belt.

When one sack was nearly full, Dad, who stood on the small platform at the rear of the thresher, moved a lever and the oats dropped into the second sack. Quickly, he

Amber waves of grain

tied the top of the full sack to safely secure the oats within. He lifted, turned slightly, and then dropped the full sack to the ground. Dad attached another sack to the machine and waited until the opposite side filled. He never had to wait long. In fact, being quick was an essential requirement for this job.

"That's a sign of a successful crop! Each sack is filling fast. All that work is paying us now," Dad bragged to himself as sacks filled, one after the other.

Some oats spilled. A burlap sack could have a small hole in it. Or a sack tipped over a little as Dad tied it. Some oats had escaped from the threshing and remained on the stalks.

You might be wondering, "Where was Clarence? Where

was Raymond? Where were my sisters? Where was I?" Well, we were not vacationing. Nor were we spending idle time playing on a pleasant late summer afternoon.

Clarence drove the truck just fast enough to keep up with the harvesting machine. Raymond, Harriet, and Carolyn walked along beside the harvester. Each took a turn, and picked up a sack and heaved it on to the truck. Often Carolyn and Harriet helped each other, for they were heavy.

When Raymond felt well, he was a fast worker. "For your size Raymond, you're surprisingly strong and fast. You look short because your brothers are so tall. You're a good average size and still growing," Dad liked to compliment Raymond when he was able to work along with the rest of us kids.

"Thanks, Dad, I'm inching my way up." With a laugh, Ray stood on tiptoes, stretched his body, and reached his arms toward the sky.

Sandy and I did our best and pushed the sacks beside one another on the truck's bed. We struggled with the sack's weight. The field was bumpy and we needed to maintain our balance as the truck rumbled along.

Raymond leapt up onto the truck and helped us stack the oats just as he had with the hay bales. "You're both a couple of weaklings! What are you doing? Just going along for a ride?" he'd say.

We didn't care what he said. He was persnickety.

That's what our dad said, "Raymond you are too per-snickety! Learn how to get along with the little kids."

At school last year, I had looked up *persnickety* in the dictionary. Dad was right. Raymond was indeed hard to please. Sandy and I never argued with Raymond.

Dad had warned, "Learn to let sleeping dogs lie." He also reminded us, "Now, two wrongs don't make a right."

When the harvesting was complete, and Dad paid Mr. Ferguson for his labor and for the use of his machinery, he helped him unhitch the tractor from the harvester. Mr. Ferguson revved up his old truck, lined the hitch on the truck with the hitch on the harvester, and Dad bolted them together. Mr. Ferguson closed the truck's creaky door, and with a wave of one arm, rumbled out of the field, and on to the dirt road. The harvester swayed from side to side as it moved over the narrow, dirt road. I heard a car horn sound as an impatient driver demonstrated his feelings about the slow-moving truck.

We arranged bag after bag of oats first on the truck and then in the barn. Clarence had driven the truck to the barn several times during that long harvesting day. The oats were stacked in long rows near the haymow, five deep rows in total. And with more sacks on top of each row, they were double decked. I thought about how many more cats we might need to keep the mice away.

Clarence was not one to waste time. "I'll get the straw raked before milking time." The oat stalks had a new name

Holsteins on a modern dairy farm enjoy forage and grains

now: straw. He drove the tractor and rake around and around the field. Soon the straw rested in neat rows.

Later, during supper Dad said, "The crows have something to crow about today. They're happy. There are plenty of spilled oats on the field."

"I hope the chipmunks eat the oats that are left behind. They need some for their winter supply, too," I answered.

The chipmunks most likely had tunneled a home into the ground underneath the rock or brush piles. Their cousins, the gray squirrels, collected oats for their winter stash as well.

The next day when the oat straw had thoroughly dried, the hay baler mashed it together section by section. Before exiting the machine, the sections were automatically tied together with tough twine just as the hay bales had been. Each newly baled straw fell onto the wagon. We kids stacked the straw bales as they popped out of the baler. Later, we stacked the straw in one of the barn's haymows.

When I watched Clarence baling the straw, I thought about that near-accident in July. "I'm a lucky kid," I told myself over and over.

And, Dad reminded us all the time, "We have so much food. Those poor kids and others all over Vermont don't have enough food or a shirt on their backs."

"Nor a pot to pee in," Raymond laughed.

I knew we were lucky.

Straw was good for many things. We spread straw in our garden to hinder the weed growth. And we used it as insulation around our home to protect the stored vegetables from the cold winds in the basement. During the long winter, straw was also used as bedding for the animals.

Sometimes the pigs ate their bedding. They'd sniff and snort and soon begin a feast. They ruined a nice clean place to take a nap. According to Dad, "Pigs will eat anything. They're just like goats."

We never had any goats but I had read stories that they ate old shoes, pieces of worn out rubber tires, and anything that fit into their mouths. Pigs ate whatever we gave them. But what we gave them was food not old tires or worn out shoes. Goats were anything but persnickety about their food!

School soon began. Sandy was in fourth grade and was happy to be seated near Johnny. "He sits right behind me and he taps me on the back with his pencil. He whispers to me during class and gets away with it. If I whisper one little word, Mrs. Abbot says, 'Turn around in your seat, Sandra!' "

"You'll have to stay in for recess if you get caught too often. You know how Mrs. Abbot is. Be careful that she doesn't get mad at you. You can whisper to Johnny when she's busy with the fifth graders," I advised. I was in the same classroom with Carolyn and Miss Flanders was our teacher.

"Pat, you'll have to do your work on time and neatly or Miss Flanders will make you do it over," Carolyn reminded me.

"I do my work on time and I'm neat, too." I sounded a little defensive. After all I was in the sixth grade!

But being back at school didn't end our work at home. There were more things to do.

"The canning factory is open for business," announced Clarence during supper one September night. "Right after school tomorrow, we'll get a start on the corn. We should be able to finish on Saturday."

"Can Pat and I go to the canning factory with you, big brother?" Sandy loved adventures just like I did.

"Oh, sure come along." Sandy and I grinned.

Chapter 18

THE CORN HARVEST

As I drove down the hill toward your father's farm, I
admired the crops growing in his large field.
John Hall, UVM Extension agent,
farmer and writer

"No one wants pasty-tasting corn. It's ready to pick," Mom said upon our return from school. "Clarence and Dad need your help out in the fields."

We girls quickly changed from our school clothes into our work clothes and headed to the cornfield.

Right after we finished with the oat harvest, we began work in the cornfield. Every day after school, we joined Clarence and Dad at work. It was important to get the harvest in because the corn was just at its correct ripeness. If it continued to mature, the taste would change from sweet and sugary to a starchy or pasty taste.

Everyone in the family pitched in to get those ears to the factory and into cans while the corn was at its perfect ripeness. Farm families all around were doing the same. We marched from cornstalk to cornstalk pulling and yanking at the ears, and heaving them onto the truck. My brother drove the truck slowly because each of us had two or three rows of corn to strip. When I was several rows away from the truck, I threw the ears with as much power as when I had thrown a baseball with Gene.

"My arm hurts," I complained to Sandy as she and I walked along yanking at the ears.

"Mine, too. I can't wait to go with Clarence to the factory."

"I wonder if we know anybody there. I'm dying to find out what it looks like inside the factory."

"Me, too," Sandy replied as we continued pulling at the ears.

Clarence stopped the truck several times to give us kids time to catch up. Finally, the ears filled the truck. Clarence delivered the corn to the Demerritt and Palmer Packing Company in Randolph about five miles away. Sandy and I rode along just as he had promised. Last year, 1953, had been a record-breaking year for the amount the factory processed. The company wanted another bumper crop this year also.

"The price of corn can drop if there is too much on the market. We don't need to break any more records this year, certainly not two years in succession." Dad understood supply and demand.

In addition to the canning factory, we sold corn to some of our vegetable customers, and we saved some for ourselves. The seasonal canning factory, built in 1906, opened for business every year in Randolph during corn-harvesting time. People from all around the Randolph area worked there.

Dad told us, "The temporary jobs at the canning factory are a bonus for many families. Even Mrs. Farnsworth has a job. Many of the seasonal workers are looking for spending money to buy things they could not otherwise afford. A television is important to some people and others are saving for a different car or money for Christmas."

"When can we have a television?" Sandy asked.

"That'll be the day when this family sits around and looks at snowy pictures in a box." Dad ruffled Sandy's hair.

"But everybody has a television. They love the television and we could watch the Lone Ranger and the Lassie shows," persisted Sandy.

"Almost all of my friends have a television. They watch it every night," I chipped in.

"Who's everybody? Who are they? We're not everybody," Dad fumed. "More people know Tom Fool than Tom Fool knows." That ended the conversation about television, at least for a while.

At the canning company, Clarence drove the loaded truck onto a large platform scale. The three of us hopped out of the cab. The corn was weighed, truck and all, by one of the seasonal workers who wrote the weight on a receipt. Then the corn was dumped onto an enormous conveyor belt.

On Clarence's first trip, the truck had been weighed by

Corn ready for harvest

itself. That weight had also been written down. Next, the seasonal worker figured out how much corn was on the truck. If you know math and had the weights of each, you could figure that out, too. The worker always gave Clarence a receipt. Clarence studied it before he tucked it into the glove compartment for safekeeping.

"Thanks, Clarence," the worker said.

Clarence nodded, "No problem Joe, thanks."

"Who's that?" Sandy wanted to know everyone.

"Joe works at the filling station. He's working to earn money for a hunting rifle." In the evening after the chores were finished, Clarence often met his friends at the Citgo station to drink root beer or Coca-Cola and shoot the breeze. Joe was one of his buddies.

The corn had traveled on the conveyor belt to the inside

of the factory. Once inside, each ear was husked by machines. The husks went off in one direction and fell right into a waiting truck. The ears were quickly steamed in huge vats, big kettle-shaped monsters that spewed and whistled noises like a giant teakettle. The corn was released from the vats, and the kernels were removed from each ear with large knife-like machines. The empty cobs moved along on another conveyor belt. They too fell into a waiting truck. We had our turn at getting both husks and cobs for our animals. Clarence had backed the truck up to the loading station at the end of that conveyor belt and the corn waste fell from the conveyor belt into the truck bed.

The steaming hot corn kernels traveled another way and fell into cans that were quickly filled, sealed, and labeled. The cans moved along a conveyor belt just like cars of a train, one following another. Seasonal workers kept track of it all, making certain that the machines operated properly.

The filled cans were packed in large cardboard boxes and stacked up. Workers loaded the boxes onto the waiting platform by the train tracks. Trains transported box after box to cities far away.

One of the seasonals, Ron, was Raymond's high school friend. He grinned at us as he gathered can after can within a wide leather strap, a dozen at a time. He held the strap tightly against the cans, picked them up with his strap, turned, and placed the contents into a cardboard box. Another worker set a piece of cardboard on top of the twelve cans. When Ron added another layer of cans, his helper quickly sealed the box and slapped a label to its top. Someone else moved the filled boxes on to a special handcart. From there they were wheeled to the dock and waited for the train. The trains transported box after box to cities far away.

Ron sported wide shoulders and muscular arms, both accentuated by his navy blue T-shirt. He reminded me of Clarence who was also very strong. Ron paused from his work for a moment, adjusted his baseball cap, and shyly remarked, "During my supper break, I open up one of these cans with my knife and eat the corn with my ham sandwiches. This corn is warm and delicious!"

We moved on, too shy to say anything. Suddenly Sandy blurted out, "He's herding cans, Patty!"

"Hey! I heard that," shouted Ron. We giggled and skipped on through the factory.

We spoke with other workers even though the noise was deafening. Most were friendly. One seasonal studied Sandy for a moment or two and with a wink asked, "Oh, you're Raymond's youngest aren't you? You're the Chase kids."

Another seasonal said, "Gosh, how I love to see your brother, Raymond, at the Hollyhock Lodge. He is as cheerful as any waiter I've met and he works so hard."

*The Demerritt & Palmer Packing Company, constructed in
1906*

Sandy proudly answered, "You should taste his apple
cider donuts!" We hurried along.

Clattering and banging came from the conveyor belts,
the steam belching from huge vats, cans clanging together, and people moving and hustling along giving each
other orders. Several people were talking all at once.

Another seasonal looked at us and glared menacingly.
"Hey, what are you little kids doing in here? This is a
dangerous place! You little kids get outa here!"

We sped on. Sandy, always with a good comeback,
poked my arm, "How does that worker know our names?
She's a grouch! I've never seen her. Have you, Patty?"

"Nope, I've never seen her anywhere in Randolph. And
I hope I never see her again," I laughed.

Sandy laughed too as we moved along. The noises seemed to say, "Move along! Move Along! Hurry up! Hurry up! Hurry up!"

As we left the factory and joined Clarence, sure enough there was Ron sitting at one of the picnic tables. While he ate his sandwich he used a spoon to dig into an opened can of corn. A bottle of Coca-Cola sat there on the table. He waved and we waved back as we hopped into the truck's cab.

"Hey, tell Raymond I'll see him at school when this work ends," shouted Ron. He waved again and returned to his meal.

"I didn't think Ron knew us," I whispered to Sandy just as Clarence opened the truck's door and hopped into the driver's seat.

"Ron knows almost everybody," Clarence replied. "He does a lot of work for someone his age. He works at the Citgo station. He meets everybody when he fills their gas tanks. He lives with his grandparents and helps them out by working a lot of different jobs. He's in high school, too."

Clarence started up the truck, released the emergency brake, switched gears, and the truck lurched forward headed toward home. We bounced over the bumpy road.

"This truck sounds like Mr. Langevin's truck," Sandy laughed.

"No way, THIS truck purrs like a kitten. It runs like a charm. That old dump truck of Bernie's is so old it creaks and is about to croak. It's on its last legs." Clarence sounded indignant.

Soon we were home. Clarence backed the truck up to the barn. The corn waste wasn't waste at all. It was food for the pigs and the cows.

"Listen to that motor!" continued Clarence just before he stilled the truck. "It runs smoothly, just like Jimmie's purr."

He began to unload the corn husks and cobs. A special lever acted as a dump truck thus making unloading easier. Clarence had seen to that.

Finally, after many trips to the canning factory all of the corn had been harvested, weighed, steamed, canned, corralled by Ron's leather strap, boxed, and made ready for a train ride.

Of course, we saved some corn for our family to use. We ate steamed corn on the cob, salted, and covered with melted butter. Mom cooked corn chowder mixed with onions, and oh, yes, potatoes, too! Sometimes carrots were added. Mom used the pressure cooker to can some of the corn in Ball jars after we removed the kernels from their cobs.

We carried the jars down the stairs to the pantry. Of course, Harriet made certain that the corn was stored together in one area.

Harriet's teacher wrote notes on her report card stating: "Harriet is respected by her classmates for her organizational skills." Now, she attended high school and Dad thought she and all of us were growing up too fast.

At home, we carried the husks and cobs to the barn in large baskets and fed them to our animals. The pigs liked the corncobs and oinked, snorted, and chewed noisily. One or two grunted some, too. Their coiled tails seemed to move in rhythm, whirling around in unison with their snorting and chewing.

The calves liked the husks. They chewed the husks with the same dreamy faraway look in their eyes as the cows when they chewed their cuds.

Clarence and Dad were not yet finished in the cornfield. The next day, a Saturday, Clarence got out the tractor and the corn chopper, another kind of machine. He drove slowly as the chopper cut and chewed up the cornstalks and spit them out into the truck's body. Dad drove the truck beside the tractor at just the same speed. Sandy and I rode with him.

We controlled the speed by saying to Dad, "Slower... no, faster...Just right...Okay!...Oops!...Now go a little faster!"

Dad laughed and winked. "You both need glasses. Now you've got me going too fast!"

Clarence's arm sometimes made a wild waving motion. The tractor and chopper could not keep up. "Hey! Slow

down! Slow down! These machines can't go any faster,"
that arm seemed to frantically call out.

When the truck was full of chopped corn, Dad drove
to the barn and unloaded it into the silo. In the silo, the
corn was called silage. It was used for food for the animals during the winter. The moisture and starches set
loose in the ground-up cornstalks fermented and the silage took on an odor - a musty, earthy smell. Cows liked
the silage. They chewed and chewed as if they were on a
pleasant summer picnic, again heads skyward, eyes partially closed with that dreamy, faraway gaze.

Soon all the cornstalks were cut, chopped, and stored
in the silo. The job was finished. What remained on the
field were very short stubby stalks, perhaps four or five
inches high, which Clarence would plow into the soil
when spring came around again. We rotated our crops.
Another year this field might be planted with potatoes, or
squash, or even oats.

Next on our task list, in early fall, was the arduous job
of harvesting potatoes. Dad became frantic because we
had to beat the weather in case of a cold snap. Weather
watching became serious.

First, Clarence had planned a special project. We needed a day or two to harvest our apples and to help Clarence with his special project.

The potatoes had to wait! We all felt a sense of hurry,
hurry! Especially Dad! But apples came first.

Chapter 19

A IS FOR APPLE

Life does not seem regular and established when there is no apple tree in the yard ... no orchards blooming in May and laden with fruit in September, no baskets heaped with the crisp smooth fruits ...
L. H. Bailey

You may have heard the expression that it takes only one rotten apple to spoil the whole barrel. A bruised apple could ruin every apple in storage. My dad encouraged us with, "Don't be rotten apples. Let's work together and get our chores started and finished on time." Another of his favorite expressions was, "Now, don't upset the applecart." When he was pleased with our efforts he'd say, "You're the apple of my eye."

"After Europeans had settled in Vermont, apples arrived by way of pomace not by Johnny Appleseed." My dad explained the story of apples in Vermont. "Pomace is the apple waste from the cider-making process. In most villages, someone built a cider mill that pressed the apples into cider. Cider mills along a river were almost as common as sawmills. Using a press, the apples were crushed and the juices squeezed out. The remains of the apples were called pomace."

Clarence nodded, "Before Vermont became a state, two

181

settlers brought a wagonload of pomace to this area. Mr. Cooley at the Vermont School of Agriculture told my class that the load was scattered on the cleared land of two farms in Randolph Center. Within fifteen years more than one thousand bushels of apples were harvested from those two farms. The apples were used to make cider, hard cider, and vinegar."

"Apples were a favorite and useful fruit in earlier times. Growers produced cider and when it ages it's called hard cider and contains alcohol. Vinegar is fermented cider and is used for preserving foods like pickles and boiled eggs. Most people liked apples, cider, donuts, pies, or other apple products just as they do today. Apples were a staple. Mr. Cooley knows a lot about apples. And, of course he reminded us that they 'can be a good moneymaker.' "

"Clarence, you listened to Mr. Cooley. When he recites history, he sounds like an encyclopedia," Dad said.

Clarence chuckled, "Old timers sat around a warm stove in the general store and sipped hard cider from a jug. That gave them something to do during idle times in the winter."

"Yes," laughed Dad, "I've had my share of hard cider as I sat with folks to catch up on the latest news. The cider kept us as warm as the heat from the woodstove."

Vinegar has a few uses. By itself it has an unsavory taste, but in addition to its preserving qualities, it is used to flavor food. Vinegar is also used as a cleanser and sanitizer and so creates a healthier and safer home. It has medicinal value as well. A little vinegar and molasses can settle an upset stomach. Whenever my dad suffered from what he referred to as his "digestive" problems, he swallowed a tablespoon of his vinegar and molasses concoction to "settle his stomach."

At one time, Dad owned an apple orchard. His apple crop was kept cool in barrels in our basement. Apples are at their best when kept at a constant temperature of about 40 degrees because, if stored at warmer temperatures, they soon become starchy, mealy, and lose their crispness. When in that vulnerable condition, any blemish on the apple can cause spoilage.

"Keeping apples in prime condition is not easy. They're finicky," Dad told us.

When he first purchased the farm, Dad brought a portion of his apple crop to the local cider mill where the mill operator processed the apples into fresh cider. The operator used a water-powered press to pulverize and squeeze the juice out. Dad paid the mill operator for his services, brought his cider home, and sold it by the gallon jug. He also sold vinegar. Eventually, Dad decided to sell his orchard. He found a local buyer, Mr. Brigham.

"Why did you sell the good apple orchard, Dad?" I asked.

"I decided to concentrate on dairy animals, our vegetable crops, and maple sugaring. It's not easy to make money with apples. Potatoes and squash aren't as finicky as apples. And maple syrup sells itself. Too many irons in the fire. Too many irons in the fire," he repeated.

On our way to school we walked past the apple orchard. A wooden sign, painted white, read: Brigham's Apple Orchard. On each corner Mr. Brigham had painted a pretty red apple with a brown curled stem and green leaf.

"That was our orchard once," Harriet had explained a year earlier, "until Dad sold it. I remember when it was sold. You little kids were just babies."

"Did you help pick the apples?" asked Sandy.

"No, I was too little. Daddy hired students from the agricultural school to help us. They were called Aggies. Part of their pay was home-cooked meals, so they ate with us during apple-picking time.

"What about our other apple orchard, Harriet?" I asked.

"The orchard near the barn was just like it is now. Daddy isn't sure if those trees were planted with seeds from pomace or by seedlings from a farm nearby."

"Why didn't Dad take care of the orchard?" Sandy asked.

"Like I said, Daddy says apples are sort of fussy. They need to be grafted and pruned to get a good crop. He needed to spray them to keep pests away. He said that one year a sudden September hail storm spoiled his apples that he had babied all summer. That made him mad."

"What kind of apples are they? How do you tell one from the other?" Sandy asked.

"I don't know all the types. But they're so old that they're called heirloom apples. I know one kind is Baldwin and they are as hard as rocks. Our Cousin Cass says they're originally from Massachusetts where she and Herb live. She calls them woodpecker apples."

"What about the others?"

Carolyn, who had quietly listened, added, "Winesaps are reddish purple when ripe, and they are the best kind for cider. Clarence told me. He also said the ones that ripen early are called Jonathans. He told me that kind is best eaten right away because they soften after they're ripe and then they wouldn't taste as good."

Soon we approached our school and joined our schoolmates in a game of softball before the bell rang.

At the end of the school day, we returned home to find Mom busy processing apple goodies. Even though the trees in the old orchard were neglected, they continued to produce fruit.

"Hi, girls! I'm making applesauce and you're just in time to help. Pat, can you rinse the rest of the apples Clarence picked today? Carolyn, you can add cinnamon and sugar to the apples that have been through the sieve. Sandy, please put the cooked apples through the sieve. Be careful not to overfill it. I'll refill the pot and boil the apples as Pat gets them rinsed. Raymond and Harriet will be home from high school soon to help."

Mom preserved some of the applesauce by packing it in waxed cardboard containers. She stored them in the freezer.

"I like the applesauce best on top of cakes and pancakes don't you Patty?" Sandy asked.

"Yeah, sure I do, but my favorite is on oatmeal with extra cinnamon sprinkled on top."

Their school day over, Raymond and Harriet came into the kitchen and marveled at the smell of cinnamon and apples.

"Best of all are Mom's baked apples!" Carolyn said. "I'll help you, Mom, bake some for breakfast."

"Good idea, Carolyn. Let's get everything ready after supper. We'll pop them in the oven in the morning. The smell of baked apples will wake everybody up."

"Oh, I wondered how early you and Mom had been up to work at that job. Now I know you guys do most of the work the night before. How do you make baked apples anyway?" I asked.

"Mom showed me how to core each apple to remove the stem and the seeds. The apple corer cannot pass through the opposite end of the apple." Carolyn continued, "I put each apple into the cake pan with a little water, cavity side up, while Mom mixes up the filling. The filling has butternuts, maple syrup, oats, flour, and lots of cinnamon mixed together. We put a little of the filling into each apple's cavity. Mom covers the whole pan with a damp towel until morning."

Early the next morning, while the apples baked in the hot oven, the aroma seeped from the oven, up the stairs, into our bedroom, and woke me.

Almost immediately I heard Carolyn's call, "Sandy! Pat! Harriet! Hey, everybody can you smell the baked apples? Get up!"

I hopped out of bed, dressed, and hurried down the stairs to the kitchen. Harriet and Sandy were close behind me.

The baked apple, with an applesauce consistency, tasted warm and sweet. The nuts, oats, and outside peel added crunch. They're good with ice cream for dessert, too.

"Mary, these baked apples are a taste of heaven on earth. And, you're the apple of my eye!" Dad complimented Mom.

One of our jobs was to peel the apples. "Hey, be careful with those knives, Carolyn. Watch what you're doing. You, too, Harriet," Mom warned.

Sandy and I got busy slicing the apples. "I'm using the guillotine first!" Sandy ran to fetch the little machine.

"And I'm next!"

"Your apple pies are the best, Harriet. I'm going to find your secret ingredient!" Raymond said admiringly. "In the meantime, I'll tantalize this hungry family with apple fritters, apple muffins, and apple cider donuts."

Gnarled apple tree in Randolph Center, Vermont

"Never," said Harriet with conviction. "I'm the only person who knows my secret and I'm not telling." Well, she had told me and I promised to never upset the applecart.

Carolyn, when out in the orchard, often said, "My pockets are full and I'm taking the best apples to Blackie." Blackie was our Angus steer.

Our dairy cows ate many of the fallen apples, called drops, as they wandered around the orchard. Sandy and I brought a few drops to the pigs in the barn mostly because we liked to watch their antics as they snorted and grunted. "Oh! What little pigs they are!" laughed Sandy.

An enormous crabapple tree stood near our vegetable garden. Sandy and I picked many of the red apples just a tad larger than the cherries we had harvested in early summer. "Pat, let's climb up there and get the rest of the apples."

Together we scurried up the tree, furiously shook a few branches, climbed down, and picked the tiny sour apples that had fallen. Our bushel basket was filling up. We grew silly while we worked and held sour-apple-face contests.

Later, Raymond teased, "You little kids should join the circus."

Sandy and I struggled to carry the filled basket to the kitchen. Mom prepared crabapple jelly. Special jars with tight lids were used. The jelly turned reddish as the peel's deep red color seeped out during stewing time. Carolyn wrote on the labels, *Crabapple Jelly 1954,* and the jars were carried to the basement and stored with the other canned goods.

Just as in former times, the pomace from our apple products had a use. Our oinkers gobbled it up snort by snort.

"The fallow trees provide good shade for our cows on a hot, summer day. Happy cows have more milk to give. Otherwise those old trees are of little use." Dad explained.

In spite of our love for the apples, our father remained oblivious to the old apple orchard and its potential use.

He overlooked any attention the trees may have needed. There they sat in the pasture until Clarence started his cider business.

Chapter 20

CLARENCE'S CIDER BUSINESS

*No idea is so antiquated that it was not
once modern. No idea is so modern that it
will not some day be antiquated.*
Ellen Glasgow

"I'm going into business. I've decided to build a cider press from all the parts I've been collecting from here and there. We've got just a few days before the potatoes need harvesting. I'll build a press in the storeroom," Clarence declared early one autumn day.

For a few evenings after chores were completed, we could hear Clarence in the storeroom hammering, sawing, and thinking out loud. When he finished, he was eager to test his skill at cider making. He needed a good supply of fresh apples from our trees. He had never made cider but we all knew that he liked to visit the cider mill owner in town.

"Son, you amaze me. You see something done once and you can do it. You see a machine and you know exactly how it works." Dad sounded proud of Clarence's skills.

"Thanks, Dad. Can you little kids give me a hand?" Clarence asked.

"Oh, yeah, what do want us to do?" we both asked.

"Help pick apples, wash them, and help with the press."

So Sandy and I took turns and climbed the one ladder we owned to harvest what we could from the trees. We scoffed up the apples that had fallen to the ground. Together we filled wooden boxes. Clarence loaded them on to the wagon and pulled them with the tractor to our storeroom. We carried the apples inside.

"I'll get some water from the kitchen tap and fill the washtub." Sandy got busy doing that. When we began rinsing the apples, many leaves, dirt, and other debris dirtied the water.

"Pat, get the water hose from the shed. These apples are dirtier than I imagined." Clarence rinsed the tub and refilled it after hooking the long hose to our outside faucet.

We separated the best-looking apples for eating out of hand, for applesauce, pies, and other goodies. Even though the apples were wild, they tasted sweet and juicy. Some were crimson red, some greenish-red with thin, red candy cane stripes. Some were small and pale yellow. Finally, they all had been rinsed.

"Clarence, do you know what kinds of apples these are?" I asked.

"The little ones are Golden Russets and the striped ones you showed me are Winesaps. The others I'm not sure. Okay, we're ready now. Let's press these critters."

Our usual Mr. Serious now became jovial as he read-ied the machine. Was he interested in cider making? Or was he more interested in testing how well his cider press worked?

Sandy and I dumped a box of apples into a funnel-like container where the apples tumbled, a few at a time, down on to the framed platform.

"Okay, that's enough apples. I'll throw the switch."

The noisy motor started. The three of us were all eyes and ears as we peered at and listened to the machine thunder into service. The top of it lowered on to a lay-er of apples. The sounds of apples being crushed, flat-tened, and mashed resounded throughout the room. Juice trickled from one end of the machine into the old ten-gallon milk can.

"Wow! That's a lot of noise!" Sandy playfully covered her ears.

"It sounds like a train crash," I shouted above the commotion.

Sandy and I continued to move the cleaned apples close to Clarence and the press. After many apples had been crushed and the pomace removed, Clarence was truly in the cider business!

I watched him as he operated the machine. His whole body seemed to be involved in his project. He leaned over the machine searching, I think, for the occasional squeak. He tweaked the rate at which the machine lowered on to the platform. He adjusted some part of it so that the top lifted more quickly after the apples were crushed. He halted the machine and carefully adjusted a couple of other parts.

Clarence sampled his product, smacked his lips, and said, "Great stuff, nice and sweet! Save that pomace for our pigs. Put it all into an empty box, Pat."

"Okay!" Sandy and I scraped the messy pomace from the machine with spatulas borrowed from the kitchen.

She and I dashed into the kitchen again for cups. We held them out for Clarence to fill.

"Clarence, this is the greatest cider! It's delicious, nice and sweet like Mr. Langevin's honey." I beamed.

"Do you have any fresh donuts?" asked Sandy mischievously.

Clarence grinned, "No, but a nickel will buy you another cup of cider!"

"Yummy! Clarence this is superb cider! It's the best you've ever made." Sandy and I giggled for it was his first, an experiment.

Clarence agreed, "Yes, it is. I'll be able to sell it. I'll ask Dad to add 'fresh cider' to his ad in the paper."

"Sandy, hold a jug and I'll fill it. No wait, this cider needs to be strained. Can you get the strainer from the kitchen, Pat?"

When I returned, I adjusted the strainer over the funnel. Sandy held jug after jug as Clarence carefully filled the containers with fresh cider using the strainer, funnel, and ladle. We repeated the process of scraping away the pomace and filling the machine's funnel with apples.

"Where did you get all of these jugs?" asked Sandy. "You have about a million!"

"Now don't exaggerate, Sandy. Dad had some stored away and Mr. Farr helped me buy some at a good price."

"Clarence, are you going to make some labels for the cider? Miss Langevin has labels for her honey jars. She draws little clover blossoms on them. You could draw apples on your labels," I suggested.

"No, not this year, but maybe someday. I'll ask Carolyn to help me with the labels."

Clarence drove his big blue Mercury around to neighbors and friends. He sold some jugs at the Citgo gas station in Randolph. After people had seen the advertisement in the newspaper, customers bought cider when they drove to our farm for Dad's vegetables.

Sandy and I carried the boxes of pomace to the pigs. As usual, the pigs ran up to us. They sniffed in the direction of the box, and peered at us between the wooden slats of their pen.

"Here, oinkers! Come oinkers," teased Sandy. "Come get your snack." Tails whirling, the pigs gazed up at us as we dumped the contents into the pigs' trough.

Heirloom apples ready for harvest

"The cider business is interesting and fun. I don't expect to make much money, not this year anyway. I've had expenses with the press, buying this and that for it. Maybe next year I'll make a little profit. I need to prune the trees this winter, graft on branches in the spring, and get a sprayer for the apples to prevent the scabby parts from growing," Clarence said later.

I knew that Clarence had made many trips to the hardware store to get needed parts for his press. I knew he had spent his own money.

"You're right, Clarence. There's no sense in doing something if you're not making money," I replied in a feeble attempt at imitating Dad. "Sandy and I can help you clean the machinery. The press will be in good working order for next year."

"Yeah, thanks. You little kids helped me a lot."

Later, when the press had been washed with soapy water and rinsed with fresh water, Sandy asked, "What's worse than finding a worm in your apple?"

"I dunno maybe two or three worms?"

"No. What is worse is finding just HALF a worm in your apple," Sandy gagged at the thought.

"Sandy, let's take some cider to school with our lunch."

"Yes, and I'll tell Johnny I know where the best cider maker in town lives." Sandy grinned.

Raymond delighted everyone by making cider donuts for dessert on that cider-pressing day. Donuts and fresh cider go together as well as pencil and paper, words to books, or hands into mittens. Too full from our dinner of pot roast, mashed potatoes, baked squash, and Raymond's coleslaw, we managed an extra donut and glass of fresh sweet cider for dessert.

The next morning hot cider and donuts greeted us at the breakfast table. "I doubled my batch yesterday and put them out of reach until now," Raymond boasted.

"You put your bakery to good use, Raymond," Clarence admired his brother's expertise as a baker.

"And, you have made good cider! Let's make this a habit." My brothers grinned at each other.

Dad smiled as he observed the budding respect between his sons. He knew these brothers were journeying on different but not opposing paths, just as Gene was finding his way.

"Please pass over that plate of donuts, Carolyn. I believe I'll have another with my coffee. We have many rows to hoe today. It's time to get those potatoes into storage. Clarence, today we begin."

"I'm ready. After the little kids helped me clean up the cider press yesterday, I had time to check the potato digger. It's out of storage, greased, oiled, and ready to go. The tractor's gas tank is full and the baskets and boxes are already piled in the field."

Dad nodded in relief. He looked all around the table at the six faces of his children, and Mom too, and took a last sip of his coffee.

Chapter 21

POTATO POTPOURRI

We all flourish or decline with the farmer.
Bernard Baruch

"We'll have to put our noses to the grindstone to get the potatoes stored without losing any to cold weather. Pray that we have no rain. Muddy potatoes do not store well," Dad worried. "Fall is here. Look at the leaves."

The harvesting season for potatoes was an extremely busy time. It began in late September almost immediately after the corn harvest. From dawn to dusk anyone home was at work in the potato field except Mom who busied herself by preparing meals for the workers. Even Raymond was out in the fields. Dad hired neighbors and students from the VSA to work for us.

Dad told all of us, "Your mother puts in a much longer workday than most of us. She's up early and the last to stoke the fires at night."

Dad worried that we were behind schedule. The weather was turning colder and our family had taken a few days to pick apples from our old orchard. "We're in a war with time and nature," Dad had explained on the first day of harvesting.

The potato harvester was yet another machine that

Clarence operated with the tractor. From a front view, the harvester looked like a miniature snowplow. Its V-shaped blades dug deep into the soil, plowed it up, and exposed the potatoes and their deep roots. The machine's conveyor belt shook loose many of the potatoes from roots deep in the soil and dropped them on to the ground behind. Once in a while the digger's blade clanged against an unseen rock. If Dad was within earshot, he cringed, and watched as Clarence quickly reversed the machinery to remove the blades from possible damage.

Every day after school my siblings and I hustled into our work clothes and headed for the seven-acre potato field. First, we gathered the dug-up potatoes that were visible. Then, we shook the sod and the roots and out rolled more potatoes for the wooden baskets. Next, they were dumped into wooden boxes and stacked on the wagon in rows, one box on top of another just as the hay bales had been.

"Pick every potato," Dad said. "There's no use in leaving potatoes for the hungry woodchucks."

Finally, the wagon was full of stacked boxes. Clarence drove the load to our house with Raymond, Harriet, Carolyn and sometimes a couple of Aggies on board. The potatoes were carried box by box down the steep stairs of our bulkhead into our basement. Carrying the filled boxes down the stairs and into the bins was creating tired muscles and short tempers. As soon as the boxes were emptied, they were returned to the wagon for refilling. Clarence had plans to build a conveyor belt during the winter. "We need to save our backs," he reasoned.

Great care was needed so the potatoes were gently dumped into the large bins. Any damaged potato would spoil, therefore ruining a great many in its wake. The root cellar was cool, dark, and moist, perfect for keeping potatoes fresh.

"Too much light will cause our potatoes to sprout. If it gets too dry or too warm, the potatoes will become soft and mealy. A wet potato will spoil, get moldy, and ruin the others around it." Dad knew a lot about storing potatoes.

Of course, during the winter there was danger that the potatoes might freeze. Two or three weeks ago, Sandy and I had helped Dad bank bales of straw and leaves along the perimeter of our house. "These straw bales and leaves will act like blankets and ward off cold winds and cold temperatures," Dad told us.

Sandy and I were too little to carry full boxes so the best place for us was in the field harvesting more spuds with Dad. He had left bushel baskets all around the field. Sandy and I filled as many as we could as we inched our way slowly along the long rows. While we worked, Sandy teased, "Pick every potato, Patty! Don't

Autumn's colors at potato harvesting time

leave a single one for the woodchucks!"

She was good at exaggerating Dad's deep voice. I could never figure out how she created a voice like that. She seemed too dainty to have such a deep voice.

"Okay, Daddy," I replied sheepishly. "You're the boss!"

We bantered back and forth while we gathered up the crop. Our conversations usually included our school life, our friends, our teachers, and our schoolwork.

"Have you seen the house where those poor kids live?" I asked Sandy.

"Yeah, it's there on the way to Mr. Adams's chicken farm. I saw it before the kids moved in."

"They still don't have any socks."

"I know, and their clothes are raggy looking. Today

Mrs. Abbott told me not to stare at them."

"Are they in your grade?"

"No. One is in the third grade and the older one is in fifth grade."

"Do they do their work?"

"Well, the little one keeps falling asleep and the teacher says, 'Wake up. This is no place to sleep.'"

I changed the subject, "It takes over four months for these potatoes to grow before we harvest them. Dad says it takes almost that long to pick them all," I giggled.

"Daddy's a kidder. That's funny!" Sandy replied.

The task of harvesting potatoes seemed to go on for weeks. In truth, the harvest took about two weeks if the weather cooperated. "This rain is putting us behind schedule," Dad fumed whenever there was a rain delay.

During the potato season, Carolyn was concerned about her schoolwork. Smart and conscientious, she always completed her assignments. She took great pride in completing her schoolwork on time and was equally as proud of her grades.

Miss Flanders often praised her. "Carolyn, you are an excellent student. Keep up the good work," Miss Flanders had written on her report card, "Carolyn has exemplary work habits and completes all assignments extremely well."

During one harvesting season, Miss Flanders directed

the class to complete a particularly long assignment. Carolyn had already started on an arithmetic assignment and now she had ten pages to read for history class.

Carolyn spoke right up, "Oh! No! I can't do all that! Today I have to pick potatoes after school. I won't have enough time. And, it's Harriet's and my turn to set the table and wash the dishes!"

"All right, Carolyn, I am excusing you from this assignment!" The teacher wrote, "C is excused" in tiny letters beside her name in her record book.

Jennie angrily confronted Carolyn during recess. They were friends and both were smart with their studies. "You're so lucky to be excused from that assignment. Now you don't have any work to do."

Carolyn replied, "Talk to the teacher; I didn't have anything to do with her decision."

Other kids said that was a lucky thing, too. They didn't know what a tedious, dirty, and time-consuming job it was to pick potatoes, I guess.

Our family ate a lot of potatoes. In addition to Sandy's favorite, mashed potatoes, we consumed baked potatoes with melted butter or sour cream. We enjoyed shepherd's pie, its top layered with crusty mashed potatoes. Boiled potatoes, boiled parsley potatoes, baked scalloped potatoes, fried potatoes, French fries, home fries with onions, and potato pancakes were all known to us. Potatoes were added to soups and chowders and combined with peas and carrots.

When Gene had been at home, he prepared French fries. Our family owned a special potato cutter. When a peeled potato was placed inside it, a lever was pushed down through the potato. The potato was cut into several pieces shaped like fat fries. Gene soaked the slices in icy water. When the potatoes were nice and crisp, he removed them and patted them dry on towels.

Gene heated our kitchen's deep-fat fryer to just the right temperature. He placed the soaked potatoes into a metal wire basket and dropped the basket into the hot oil. The oil sizzled and cooked the fries until they were brown and crispy.

"I love your French fries! Gene will you make us some?" Sandy asked.

"Okay, kiddo. That's all I know how to make." He set to work at his favorite and only kitchen task.

When his baseball buddies visited after a game, they gathered in the kitchen and prepared fries for a snack. From my bedroom, I could hear Gene talking about the Brooklyn Dodgers and their latest deeds.

"Have you seen that picture in the newspaper of Pee Wee Reese stretching to make that catch?" Or, "Another home run for Jackie!" Or, "Roy Campanella what a catcher he is! He's the best ever!"

One of his friends agreed and added, "Johnny Pedros

is the team's best pitcher."

"Gene, do you have any vinegar? You know I like vinegar on my fries," asked one friend. I heard Gene searching through the cupboards for vinegar.

"Try the fries with ketchup," another friend suggested. "This isn't John's Diner."

Before we finished the potato harvest, Clarence, Sandy, and I anticipated a special adventure. We were going to a very special place where Raymond had told us, "You'll have the time of your life! Bring your money!"

Dad decided, "All right you can go with Clarence, Pat. Uncle Jim will help us by doing Clarence's job in the fields."

"Can I go, Daddy? Please, can I go?" asked Sandy.

"Let's see, Pat needs to win first prize for her 4-H Club first. Then we'll talk about it."

"I'm going! I'm going! I know Patty will win." Sandy danced and squealed with joy when she heard Dad's decision.

After the chores were finished that day, and evening had begun, Sandy continued to talk about her expectations at the fair. "I really want to go, Patty!"

"I need to win first, Sandy, so don't get all worried about it. Let's play a game of Pick Up Sticks."

"Yes!" Sandy ran to the cupboard and lifted the long cylindrical box that held the game. We dumped the long sticks out on the table.

Raymond E. Chase (highlighted in third row),
VSA graduation. 1922

"I'm first!" Sandy said.

"We should follow the rules for who starts first, but okay, this time you go first," I agreed.

"We must beat the weather. We're headed for a cold snap. It's time to batten down the hatches." Dad always had an eye on the weather.

Chapter 22

THE 4-H CLUB

*It is the simple things of life that make living worthwhile,
the sweet fundamental things such as love and duty, work
and rest and living close to nature.*
Laura Ingalls Wilder

Carolyn, Harriet, and I were members of the 4-H Club, a program for youth sponsored by the University of Vermont Extension Program. Sandy was too young but in another year she could join. Many of my friends were 4-H members. The 4-H logo consisted of a four-leaf clover with an H on each leaf. The letters H symbolized: Head, Heart, Hands, and Health.

As 4-H Club members, we believed in the 4-H motto: To Make the Best Better. Our meetings were held at the Vermont School of Agriculture. At every meeting we recited the 4-H pledge. It went like this and still does.

*I pledge my Head to clearer thinking
my Heart to greater loyalty,
my Hands to greater service,
and my Health to better living,
for my club, my community, my country,
and my world.*

"That's an excellent belief system for anyone," Dad declared. "That's as good as saying, 'God helps those who help themselves.'"

Our leader was Mr. Cooley who had grown up on a near-by farm and had gone to college. His dad was a teacher at VSA. The 4-H Club offered its young members many fun activities and learning opportunities. We chose activities that pleased us.

"I'm choosing the dairy group and the gardening group. I'll grow a big pumpkin, the largest in Randolph. And Suzie, the calf Dad gave me, will win blue ribbons."

"I want to learn more about chickens so I'm joining the poultry group," Harriet decided.

Harriet and Carolyn both chose crafts and sewing. Mom had taught them how to sew their own clothing, and my older sisters wanted to look stylish and hip.

Mr. Cooley said, "I like your choices. I don't know much about sewing but I can find you girls some help from the county extension office. And perhaps your mom can give us a hand."

I raised a Holstein calf given to me by my dad. As he passed the young calf over to me, he reminded me of the responsibility of caring for the animal. Of course, I had learned all about the care and needs of animals.

"Yes, I'll feed and water my calf every day," I assured him. "Yes, I'll clean her pen regularly and place clean straw in it so that she rests comfortably."

I named my calf Suzie. She was a beautiful animal with shiny black and white markings and big, bright, black eyes. I kept my agreement with my dad. And I brushed her regularly to keep her coat clean and shiny. I gave her fresh water, grain, and hay as she grew. I liked to pet her and she liked to have her neck scratched. Her head sported a perfect white-shaped heart surrounded by black velvet-like fur. To me, she looked perfect.

Mr. Farr visited our farm regularly to see my father and Clarence. He noticed Suzie.

"Suzie is a fine-looking animal. She has the features of a registered Holstein." Turning to me he continued, "Suzie's heart-shaped forehead makes her a winner."

Father laughed and asked, "Okay, but how much milk will she produce when she's full grown?"

Clarence chipped in, "Her sire is a registered Holstein. When Suzie calves, she'll produce a good-looking animal because she'll be bred with pure Holstein serum."

A registered cow has special characteristics and is bred from particular bulls that are pure Holsteins. The cows resulting are usually good milkers and look special because they have good bone structure. Their backs are straight not sway-backed. Most important, they are a pure breed, which means they are a hundred percent Holstein for several generations. When grown up, their udders are larger than those not registered and thus they often produce more milk. It is for those reasons that a registered animal has more value.

Our dairy herd was a good one but it was not a regis-

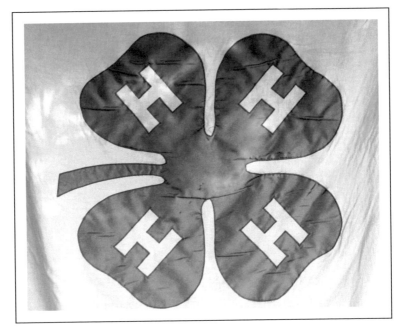

Banner with the 4-H logo

tered herd. As a student, Clarence began to keep records of each cow's sire so he could prove that each future generation of the herd was bred with pure Holstein serum. He had learned the benefits of owning a registered herd at the VSA.

"Our herd is moving in that direction. Soon we'll have a registered herd like the Howe farm," Clarence said.

I taught Suzie how to follow my lead with a halter. I taught her how to stop, how to keep her head up, and how to keep her legs just so.

Dad praised me. "Pat, you've trained Suzie to behave in the ring. That will impress the judges. The judges will be able to get a good look at her. They will notice her straight back, good bone structure, and a balanced body on strong, sturdy legs."

I led Suzie around the field near our barn. I stopped her by using one special pull on her halter. When it was time to resume walking, I gave another tug on the halter just a little different. I practiced and practiced with her. I rewarded her with an apple or a little grain. Lassie tagged along with us.

"Animals are able to learn when you repeat things many times. Be patient with them and don't hurt them. Treat them as best friends," Mr. Cooley taught me.

At times like this, I remembered the lessons in the book about Black Beauty, the horse that survived a succession of many different owners. The laboring horse pulled carriages, carts, and wagons on busy city streets in England long ago. He had been treated sometimes with fairness, kindness, and at other times with cruelty and disdain by various owners. I always treated Suzie with kindness.

When the local 4-H Day arrived I led Suzie to the Vermont School of Agriculture that was located less than a mile from my home. I walked with her taking the shortcut through the pastures and Mr. Brigham's apple orchard and arrived at the school right on time. My 4-H friends in the dairy group were already there with their animals.

"I won! I won!" I shouted to my family when I returned home later that afternoon. "I won! You should have come with me, Sandy. I can go to the Tunbridge Fair with Suzie because she won the blue ribbon. Come with me, Sandy! I hope Dad says you can come, too."

"He said so, didn't he? Didn't he say yes?"

"Not exactly, Sandy. He said he'd think about it if I won the ribbon. Well, I've won a blue one. We need to ask Dad again. He said Clarence and I can go if I win."

"Clarence will bring us. We helped him with his apples. Maybe he'll ask Daddy for me."

"It's better if you ask him, Sandy. I'll go with you when Dad is reading the paper."

"Are you sure? You ask him, Patty. Please!"

"Oh, all right. Dad knows I wanted to win and maybe now I can win another. I'll ask him if you can come. I'll tell him I need your help with Suzie's halter, her water, and grain."

"Just tell him I want to go. I'm sick of picking those old cold potatoes. My hands are like ice cubes from the cold. I've never been to the fair either. It's about time I get to go there."

Our strategy was set. Later, Sandy and I approached Dad as he began a relaxing evening with his paper.

"Dad, do you think Sandy can go to the Tunbridge Fair with Clarence and me? Please? I need her help and she really wants to go."

Dad put aside his paper and looked at me. Then he looked at Sandy and cleared his throat. "Of course, Pat. It's all set. Uncle Jim is going to do Clarence's job in the fields and Raymond, Harriet, and Carolyn will pinch hit for you little kids."

Sandy shouted a "Yahoo!" and began a dance near Dad's desk. "Thank you, Daddy. Thank you."

Dad messed up her hair, smiled, and returned to his newspaper.

The Tunbridge Fairgrounds has an area of fields, sheds, barns, and other buildings used for exhibits. Various meetings and area conventions are held there at different times of the year. But the most popular event at the fair-grounds is the Tunbridge World's Fair held every fall. And that is when I brought Suzie to Tunbridge. The fair has been held every year since 1867, almost a hundred years. Every year Sandy and I had yearned to go. In 1954, our chance had finally come.

Clarence promised me, "Don't worry, Pat. I'll get you there. Sandy too."

Raymond had been to the Tunbridge Fair. He played the trumpet in the high school band and the band had played on the grandstand stage last year.

"We're playing again this year, too," Raymond bragged to Sandy and me. "Take the ride of your lives! Get on the Ferris wheel. You'll love it. You'll see the fairgrounds all at once like a bird in the sky. I've been on it with Brenda, Butch, and other kids in the band."

"How much money does it cost?" I asked.

"Oh, Pat, never mind the cost. You've got money. You

little kids have money. Don't be tightwads. Just buy tickets and wait in line. Everybody goes on the Ferris wheel."

Sandy and I talked about it. We each decided to bring a whole dollar of our allowance with us.

Clarence figured out a way to transport Suzie safely in the back of our truck. He built a tight-fitting pen and nailed it down on the truck's floorboards to prevent it from moving while the truck was in motion. With that arrangement Suzie could not fall and injure herself during the long ride. Tunbridge was about fifteen miles from our farm, which was a long way for an animal to ride in the back of a truck. Part of the way was over a bumpy, little-used gravel road.

Clarence practiced leading Suzie into the pen with a length of rope. He wanted her to grow accustomed to being there. He left her there for a while so she'd feel safe.

"Let me put Suzie in the pen, Pat. She won't think you are to blame for her squeezed-in feeling. I'll take her out of the pen when we get there, too." Clarence liked animals as much as I did.

On the day of the show, I was as excited as a cat pouncing on a newfound mouse. Just as he had practiced, Clarence dropped the tailgate of the truck that formed a ramp. He placed a rope around Suzie's neck and led her up the ramp into the small pen. He tied the rope securely to the front of the pen with a little slack.

"Now, Suzie will be able to move her head just a bit," Clarence said. "Let's go!" We were off.

About a mile from our home, Sandy nudged my arm. "That's the shack where those kids live."

"Look, they have one window that's stuffed with old rags because the pane is broken." I stared at the rags and the cracked glass as we passed by.

"I wonder what it looks like inside. We're lucky, Patty. Our house is so big. Their house looks like one tiny room."

"They'll be moving on soon. That old shack is on the Moore farm. The people don't have permission to stay there." Clarence sounded a little worried.

"Where will they go?" I asked.

"Do they have a father?" Sandy asked.

"I don't know. I'm not sure. Some people in town are looking for a place for them." Clarence sped up a little and slowed down again to dodge a couple of potholes.

Sandy and I rode in the truck cab with our feet resting on Clarence's toolbox. We were both eager. I wore my white shirt and white pants. I brought Suzie's halter, her brush, grain in a paper bag, and a bucket for water for that animal with the heart-shaped forehead.

We reached the fairgrounds and there before us sat the magical place.

Sandy nudged my arm. "Look! There's the Ferris wheel. Raymond's right. It's so high. It's so big! I can't wait for a ride!"

She and I stared in wonder at the Ferris wheel.

Chapter 23

SWEETHEART OF THE TUNBRIDGE FAIR

Nothing great was ever achieved without enthusiasm.
Ralph Waldo Emerson

Clarence opened the tailgate and when I saw Suzie, I could tell she was nervous. Her liquid eyes held a frightened gaze as she peered at us from her pen. Clarence gently untied Suzie, backed her out of the narrow pen, and led her down the tailgate and into the barn to a pen in one corner. "It's all right, Suzie," he whispered, petting her. My brother removed her rope, and I quickly put on her halter.

I quieted her and briefly walked her outside. Back in the barn, I offered Suzie water and grain. I brushed her fur. Suzie had calmed down and drank a little water.

All around us were other kids with their animals, mostly Holsteins, Suzie's competitors. There were a few Jerseys, a different category, and a couple of Guernseys made up another group.

"You little kids go look around at the sheds and barns for a while. I'll stay with Suzie," Clarence suggested.

Off we went. One building specialized in horses, the working category, and the breed for riding. A shed sheltered sheep and others housed pigs. One old building contained chickens.

"Harriet would like seeing these chickens," I thought out loud to Sandy. She agreed. "Look at all these special areas for the pets. There are kittens, cats, rabbits, dogs, and puppies." They were in search of good homes. "Look at all the little kitties, Sandy. They're so cute."

"Come on, Patty. Let's go. We see kittens all the time. Let's go over to that building."

In a building nearby, many items entered by 4-H kids were on display. There was an area for cakes, pies, cookies, maple fudge, maple syrup, and honey, all to be judged for their quality.

"Oh, Patty all this food makes me hungry." Sandy rubbed her tummy.

"Me, too," I said. "Raymond packed us sandwiches."

"I don't want any old sandwiches," complained Sandy.

Another area had sewn items for inspection. Things like cotton napkins, colorful tablecloths, handkerchiefs, and clothing were there.

"Harriet and Carolyn should have entered their new skirts and blouses. Sandy, look at the skirts with little poodles on them."

"Neat!" Sandy exclaimed. "I love those poodles!"

Knitters showed off their handiwork with scarves and mittens.

"Here's some knitting stuff that looks like things Aunt Almira makes." Sandy lifted each scarf and pairs of mittens. "Wow! I like this color!"

Another area displayed woodworking items including duck decoys and whittled whistles. Small pieces of artwork were there including paintings, drawings, and posters.

Another table showed off vegetables including all types of squash, potatoes, and pumpkins.

"Look! Those are the largest pumpkins I've ever seen," I exclaimed. "The pumpkins I planted didn't do this well. They hardly grew."

"Raymond could make a lot of pies with them. Wow! Look at that one over there!" Sandy pointed to a giant gourd.

One or two tables were filled with garden vegetables such as carrots, tomatoes, turnips, beets, and beans.

Nearby sheds protected the latest farm equipment for sale. Brand new tractors, hay rakes and balers, shiny watering bowls, sparkly new milking machines, plows, cultivators, and potato harvesters were lined along the back wall. There was the latest in maple sugaring equipment for us to inspect: shiny evaporators, gathering tanks, holding tanks, gathering pails, spouts, buckets, lids, and variously designed syrup containers.

"Look, Sandy I'm going to tell Clarence about this building. There's a battery-operated drill. He'll be able to tap our trees really fast. And look over there at the tractors and bulldozers. And there are some watering bowls."

Clarence had been talking with Dad about the need for watering bowls in the cows' mangers. "Just think, Dad. The cows can get the benefits of watering bowls just like at VSA. They can take a drink whenever they're thirsty. They'll be happier and give more milk. All we need to do is buy the bowls and the pipes. I can put them together myself to save on costs. I'll connect the pipe to the faucet in the milk house."

Dad was thinking about it. Mr. Farr had been talking about watering bowls with Dad, too. Clarence knew that soon his dad would be making an important purchase to improve the efficiency of the farm, the health of the cows, and most likely increase the milk check.

We could see the midway where some booths were beginning to open. Food booths, game booths, and the rides were located here. The Ferris wheel stood high above everything.

"We'll ride on that, Sandy. When the judging is finished, that's the first thing we'll do," I promised.

"Okay, Patty. I hope you win another blue ribbon. I am so excited about riding the Ferris wheel I can't wait!"

Sandy danced along the lane a step or two ahead of me on our way back to Suzie.

Later, after the judging and when everything opened

for the day, we'd have more time to roam around. Although we had never been to the fair, we had heard about it and read about it. Raymond, of course, had told us about the fair.

Back at the barn Clarence assured me. "Suzie is calm. But stay with her to keep her spirits up. Be careful with your money. I'll get us a snack."

He set off to get some food. Clarence had been here before. He knew which food booths were likely to open early.

"Hey, Clarence, there are some bulldozers over that way. And some watering bowls." I pointed.

"Oh, I'll take a look later. I'll be right back." He repeated, "I'll buy some snacks."

"Okay, then," I replied.

Clarence returned with donuts and drinks. I was too anxious to eat a donut, but thanked him for the orange soda.

Sandy said, "Pat, I'll eat your donut for you!"

Now it was show time! 11 am! Clarence and Sandy left the barn to sit on the bleachers near the show ring.

"Hurry, Clarence! The bleachers are filling up fast. We need a good seat. Hurry!" Sandy exclaimed.

When I brought Suzie out of the barn and into the ring, both she and I were edgy and nervous. My eyes squinted as I faced the hot sun. It was a glorious autumn day. I noticed that all around us were hills and trees with

Award-winning corn

leaves of many colors and the little town, also on a hill, edged its way along one side of the fairgrounds.

The judges asked people to quiet themselves so that the animals would settle down. Suzie relaxed. One judge was a woman and two were men. I led Suzie around the designated ring two or three times following the other 4-H kids. Because Holsteins were the favorite breed for many Vermonters, there were many in the ring.

The judges then directed each 4-H member and her Holstein into the center of the ring forming a line facing the audience in the bleachers. Suzie had calmed down and stood just as I had taught her. I didn't know any of the other kids there; the show included all the Orange County 4-H clubs.

The judges looked over each animal carefully. One judge peered at Suzie's forehead and whispered, "That's a beautiful heart shape there on that animal's head, a perfectly shaped heart. How did she get that?"

"Mr. Farr says he likes it too," I stammered. The judge petted Suzie on her white heart surrounded by the sleek black fur, winked at me, and moved to the next animal.

Soon the judges began distributing the ribbons. The judges distributed the white ribbon first. Blue, red, pink, and white were the order of the ranking colors. Only blue ribbon winners could move on to the state contest.

The white ribbon was distributed first. One of the judges walked over to a boy at the end of the row. The boy, although smiling, seemed a little disappointed. His Holstein was registered. Registered animals won Blue Ribbons almost always. The audience politely clapped.

One of the judges walked toward me with the pink ribbon. Smiling, she attached the light pink ribbon to Suzie's halter. I stared at the pink ribbon. Clarence, Sandy, and others clapped. I waved.

Then a bright red ribbon was placed on the halter of another animal. The calf's owner, Joanne, shrieked with excitement, jumped up and down, and waved to her family. Her sunglasses fell to the ground. I wished that I owned sunglasses. She kissed her Holstein between its eyes and glowed with pride.

I eyed the boy with a crew cut next to me as a royal Blue Ribbon was secured to the Holstein's halter. My envy showed. I swallowed hard. He smiled with satisfaction, petted his animal, and waved to his family on the bleachers. They waved back and clapped proudly. He glowed with pride. His animal was registered.

Before we left the arena, everyone on the bleachers clapped. As I led Suzie back to the barn, Clarence and Sandy left the bleachers and followed me.

"A pink ribbon, Pat! That's my favorite color. It's so pretty! Hey, what did that judge say to you?" Sandy spoke fast and excitedly.

"He said, 'Here's the sweetheart of the Tunbridge Fair'!" We giggled as I editorialized a bit.

There was time to see other parts of the fair before we returned home. Clarence reminded us about the usual things like watching our money and being careful.

"Here's a peanut butter and jelly sandwich for each of you. Raymond packed them for us. Suzie's okay here. Don't worry about her. I'll meet you up there on that knoll. I'll be there in two hours, so Pat, check your watch. Look around the midway first and go up there last."

He pointed to the hilly area. "And take that ride on the Ferris wheel. Do what Raymond suggested! Don't disappoint him."

Pat with Suzie (milkhouse and barn in background)

"We will!" we both said at once.

Clarence and some of his friends who had driven over to Tunbridge headed toward the midway. I petted Suzie and gave her a hug. Sandy and I left the barn. Suzie was safe. She had water to drink, grain to eat, fresh straw upon which to rest, and a pink ribbon.

"Let's go! I can't wait any longer!" exclaimed Sandy.

Sandy's crazy dance movements and the glee on her face were evidence of her excitement and anticipation of what lay ahead. We headed for the midway at a run. I jammed my peanut butter and jelly sandwich into my pocket. Our pace slowed to a walk as we encountered people along the midway.

Chapter 24

SQUASH GALORE

You know, someday you will outgrow being little.
Being little does not last long. We all start out that way.
My father, Raymond E. Chase

The Tunbridge Fair had come and gone. Suzie won a ribbon. Sandy and I feasted on hot dogs, soda, cotton candy, and fudge. Clarence treated us to ice cream.

We loved the Ferris wheel. Round and round we flew. Just as Raymond had predicted, we were higher than we had ever been.

The one-room schoolhouse, rickety and ancient, made us realize how lucky we were to have a three-room schoolhouse, with extra space for a cloakroom, a kitchen with tables, and running water.

Sandy elated in seeing the square dancers. "One of the dancers grabbed my hand and we twirled round and round. The fiddle music was a fast beat and I loved it!"

***

"It's not fair! I can't do this, I can't do that and it's just because I'm little. That's not fair, is it, Daddy? I'm old enough to use a knife," fumed Sandy.

"Sandy, don't forget, we did go to the Tunbridge Fair," I reminded her.

Dad looked up. "You'll grow soon enough," he said and

then returned to his paper.

As soon as the potato harvest ended the squash gathering began. Dad continued in a race to beat the cold weather. A freeze had been predicted and the squash needed to be gathered and stored in the root cellar right away.

I had watched Dad cut summer squash from their vines so I knew how to handle a knife and cut each kind of squash. The vines caused my hands to itch. I had to have my gloves handy. If I didn't wear gloves, a nasty, itchy red rash developed. That required a strong prescription lotion to repair the damage.

Dad always cautioned, "Be careful with that knife! And wear your gloves, Pat."

"Okay, Dad," I hurriedly removed my pocketed gloves, covered my hands, and set to work.

Dr. Woodruff said that, like Raymond, I suffered from allergies. "Pat needs to use this medication on her hands when she is working with squash, beans, or any other vine-type plant. Better yet, she needs gloves when at work."

Raymond was allergic to chalk dust, dirt, hay, straw, and animal fur. He was bothered by what Mom called the sniffles. Sinus infections and headaches plagued him.

With great fanfare Raymond often said, "I'm allergic to this house, that old dirty, nasty barn, the hay in the fields, straw, animal fur, and the chalk at school. I have no place to call home and no school to go to! And, I'm allergic to you little kids!"

"And we love you, Raymee, don't we Patty?" Sandy teased.

Raymond was a joker. He always made his comments with a wry grin and surveyed his audience to be certain we were laughing with him not at him. He was clever that way. "You have a good sense of timing with your punch lines, son," Dad told him.

The tractor pulled the wagon slowly along the field as we lifted each squash and gently placed them up on the wagon.

When I grew tired of cutting the tough stems from their vines, I handed my knife over to Dad. I joined Sandy on the wagon and placed the squash into wooden boxes after they were placed up on to the wagon by Harriet, Carolyn, and Raymond. As we collected them, Sandy and I kept our balance as we lurched slowly along. Soon many boxes were full.

Raymond jumped up on the wagon and helped with the stacking. Sandy and I were too little to lift a full box by ourselves. We tried but they were too heavy. Each one weighed a ton. Just kidding!

Clarence had warned, "If you're going to help, keep your balance. Don't fall off and get hurt."

When Raymond gave us a hand he mumbled, "You're both a couple of weaklings. What makes you think you can do this work?" Then he'd laugh as if he had just said the funniest thing in the world.

We didn't care what he said. Sandy and I kept right on doing all that we could. We never allowed Raymond to annoy us. With a quick glance at each other or a nudge on the arm, she and I affirmed our place in the family. We'd laugh to please him. We were the "little kids," of that there was no doubt.

Sandy mumbled to herself, "It's not fair, Patty."

Dad often remarked, "Never let anyone pull the wool over your eyes." He wanted us to watch out for each other.

Sometimes Dad had made the job easier for all of us. He would be out in the fields while we were at school. He would cut the squash from the hairy vines and pile them along the edges of the mounds. There, they were more easily gathered up and placed in boxes.

Back at our house, the squash were stored in their correct bins. Everyone carried boxes of squash down the stairs and into the basement. That was hard work and the boxes, like I said, were too heavy for Sandy and me. So, she and I carried a squash, one at a time, down the bulkhead stairs into the basement and into their correct bins.

We sold the squash in the same way as the potatoes. People came to our house to buy them or my father delivered them to their homes. They were sold by size: small, medium, or large. That was all the separation that had to be done. With potatoes that was a little different because they were sold by the pound, usually a bushel, half bushel, or a peck at a time. My father used special containers somewhat like brown paper grocery bags of many different sizes. He also used heavy woven burlap sacks. People brought the sacks back when they returned to buy more potatoes.

Some of my friends didn't like squash of any kind because they said it was too mushy. But not our family. Our family ate baked squash sprinkled with butternuts and topped with maple syrup or honey to sweeten the taste. Mom flavored squash soup with cut-up pieces of potatoes with onions, apples, and carrots.

Mom crafted "dinner in a Hubbard." A big Hubbard squash cut in half with its seeds removed created a perfect baking dish. A mixture of ground beef and spices similar to meatloaf was placed inside each half. After baking in two large pans with a little water, the squash served as both vegetable and protein. Mom or Raymond baked squash pies and pumpkin pies for our Thanksgiving dinner.

When we grew pumpkins, we put a few on our steps a week or so before Halloween.

"Pat, this is the biggest pumpkin. It makes a great jack-o'-lantern." Sandy's arms could barely go around it.

"You should've taken this pumpkin to the fair, Patty."

"I couldn't take that one. Remember, I planted my pumpkin seeds near the rhubarb patch."

"Oh, that's right." Sandy nodded.

"I've chosen this one. I'll get some knives from the kitchen."

Mom was in the kitchen and noticed me. "Sandy cannot use knives, you know that."

"We're only cutting up old pumpkins to make a jack-o'-lantern. Sandy says it's not fair."

"You heard me. Sandy can't use knives."

"Oh, all right." I left the kitchen with one knife. Quickly I cut the hat for each pumpkin from its stem. Sandy quickly hollowed out the seeds. "Sandy, ask Mom for the candles." She returned with them.

Sandy used a pencil to sketch two eyes, a nose, and a crooked mouth on each pumpkin. Carefully, I carved each from the pumpkin. Then we used a little clay to hold a candle in place in the pumpkin's cavity. During Halloween, we would light the candles, set the jack-o'-lanterns on the porch, and watch their glow far into the evening.

After Halloween, we cut the remaining pumpkins open and removed the seeds. The seeds were food for the pigs.

Sandy and I left a few seedy remains of pumpkins or squash near our raspberry patch for our small friends, the chipmunks, the gray squirrels, and the cottontail rabbits.

"The mice will eat most of those seeds because they're faster than the other animals," Dad advised.

"Okay," we replied. But we didn't want to believe him. We paid little attention and continued the practice.

Tan butternut squash

The pumpkins were also cut up into quarters and boiled in water. When it had cooled, the pumpkin mass was removed from the shell. This pumpkin pulp was used for soups, pies, and other baked goods. The pumpkin shells? Well, you know where they went.

Raymond baked both pumpkin and squash pies. He added sugar, spices, milk, and what he called his "secret" ingredient. In fierce competition with Harriet, he had his own set of secret ingredients.

"MOST of your secrets are in that old cookbook you use all the time, Ray," Harriet always kidded.

Mom used a recipe to make a spicy pumpkin cake. That was odd because most of her cooking was accomplished by using her eye. She almost never opened a recipe book.

"When you cook as much as I do, your eye can tell you when the ingredients are just right."

"But how will I know without a recipe?" Ray asked.

"Like I said, your eye will tell you."

Raymond scratched his head and insisted, "But you need a recipe!"

The pumpkin cake was terrific with whipped cream. Guess who whipped up the best and tastiest whipped cream? If you think Raymond, then you are right! If you think Carolyn, you're right! Or if you think Harriet, you're also correct!

"With all this wonderful food, we have no need to go to John's Restaurant for a meal," Dad said one evening.

"I want to go to that restaurant. When can I go there and order food I want?" Sandy asked.

"Yeah, at the fair, we ordered hot dogs in a bun and just like that, they were served to us," I chipped in.

"The price you paid for one hot dog could buy a whole package for everyone. It's too expensive to go to a restaurant," Dad answered. And that ended that conversation for a while.

Sandy and I were banned from the cooking details of our household during food prep time.

"You little kids get out from underfoot," bigger people told us when we were in the kitchen.

"It's not fair!" said Sandy. "Everybody else gets to go into

Pumpkins ready for harvest

the kitchen any old time they want. It's not fair, is it Pat? It's not fair!"

My dad consoled us, "You know someday you will out-grow being little. Being little does not last long. Enjoy be-ing little. We all start out that way. You will always be the youngest among us but not the smallest or littlest."

Dad reached for Sandy and placed one of his large hands on one of her cheeks. He smiled at her. Then with his other hand, he reached over and tousled my hair. We both were the apples of his eye.

It was hard for me to imagine my father as a boy who had started out little. It was difficult to think that one day Sandy and I would be grown-ups.

Chapter 25

GRADING POTATOES

Life is what we make it. Always has been. Always will be.
Grandma Moses

"Pat, it doesn't matter. When your teacher tells you to do something, it needs to be done. It's your job to do whatever she says. The teacher isn't wrong. How many kids are in your classroom anyway? Miss Flanders can't spend every minute listening to your reasons for this or for that! She's there to teach you to read and write. That's her job," Dad reminded me when I complained about school or some kids in my class.

Dad helped me sort things out. He told me what the teacher was supposed to do and he explained what I was expected to do at school as he sorted potato after potato. He answered my complaints with words that Raymond referred to as "one of his lectures."

I sometimes trekked to the basement with Dad on evenings when he had given up reading the newspaper until he had graded a few bushels of potatoes. He spent time sorting potatoes by quality. The finest ones were saved for reseeding our fields for another year, or they were sold as seed potatoes to people who planted their own crop. Other potatoes were sold by the bushel or peck, after they were graded.

Potatoes left our home all year. Our customers bought either the best quality or the seconds. Usually, Dad added a few extra pounds to the sacks of seconds. Mostly large families or poor people bought the seconds.

"They have a lot of children to feed," Dad would say, or "They're poor, work hard, and don't have much."

"Dad, do you know those kids who lived in that old house down by the Moores?" I asked. "Well, they're not in school anymore."

"Well, they wouldn't be, would they?"

"What do you mean? What happened to them?" I asked.

"They're better off where they are now. They were staying in a shack that didn't belong to them. They couldn't stay there any longer."

"Why not, they weren't hurting anybody, were they?"

"Pat, you can't just move in wherever it suits you. What would we do if someone moved into our horse barn, for example?"

"I don't know. What happened to them? Where have they gone?"

"Don't worry. They're in Barre with relatives. They're better off there. They have two extra rooms for them."

"Are they okay? Where will the kids get some food? I am worried about them."

"Pat, there's no need to worry. The Parent Teacher Association decided at their last meeting to collect food and clothing for them. The Bigelows found someone from the Rotary Club to drive them to Barre. They'll be all right once they get settled down. There are poor people everywhere. The town's public welfare probably helped them, too."

"Did we give them some stuff?"

"Clarence and Raymond gave them cider, potatoes, carrots, and squash. Mom gave them clothing Sandy had outgrown."

"Nobody talked to them at school. They never wore any socks," I said.

"Do you remember the day you went to the fair?" Dad asked.

"That was my best day ever." I smiled thinking about the Ferris wheel.

"Well, when all the chores were done on that day, Clarence drove his car around to friends to sell his cider. He also left some with the squatters. He brought along some of Mother's bread, a jug of milk, and some vegetables, too. Clarence is a kind soul."

"What are squatters? Clarence didn't tell me he went there. What does that place look like inside?"

"Squatters are people who live where they're not supposed to be. Your brother, he's a doer, and not a talker."

As we talked, Dad used a machine with a crank on one side to grade the potatoes. They filled a large bin-like box at one end of the grader. When he turned the crank, the rollers on the machine moved the potatoes so he could spot and select the best ones. He placed them in a basket and later gently dumped them into a sack. He weighed the full sack to make sure it contained just a bushel, no more, no less. His estimate of a bushel was usually within a pound or two. Finally, he tied the sack with a piece of tough twine and placed it in the special area for the premiums along with the seed potatoes that had been separated. These were the most expensive.

At one time, Dad had used special tags showing his name and the potatoes' quality. Fine pieces of wire held the tag to each sack. The tag said:

RAYMOND E. CHASE FARM
RANDOLPH CENTER, VERMONT
GREEN MOUNTAIN POTATOES
PREMIUM QUALITY

"Everyone knows I sell potatoes. There's no longer a need for tags. And, it's one less thing to worry about."

The remaining potatoes were the seconds. I gathered them up on the opposite side of the grader and placed them in boxes. Later they, too, were placed in sacks and weighed. Well, the seconds were over-weighed. The sacks were tied with string and placed in their area.

Dad warned, "No one will buy our potatoes if the seconds get mixed up with the premiums."

The premiums were perfect potatoes, nice big ones with

no cuts or spoiled parts. Seconds were potatoes turned partially green by exposure to the sun. Or the harvesting machine could have nicked a potato. Or a potato might have spoiled parts. Some might have diseased skin or a discolored rough part. Others might be too puny, the size of a grape. The worst of these were tossed into an old pail and classified as unfit for sale and fed to the pigs.

"Pretend every premium is for Mrs. Avery's baking oven. She loves an oval-shaped potato not a round one. They all taste the same, nice white Green Mountain potatoes but she's more particular about the shape of her tubers than the taste. We'll hear about it if she's not satisfied." Dad winked.

Dad used the truck and delivered potatoes to our larger customers, Mrs. Hogdon's Rooming House and Norwich University in Northfield. Other customers lived in the Randolph area. He also delivered potatoes to families, or they drove to our farm to pick them up.

It was very important to my father to keep Mrs. Avery and all our customers satisfied. "Dad's a good salesman and a good public relations type of guy," Mom had said.

The one good thing about working with Dad was that I got to talk with him about school and other things on my mind. Sometimes one or two kids, even Bobby, called me unpleasant names like "tree trunk" or "stubby legs."

I'd reply back, "Well, you're a dummy, you can't read!"

Dad cautioned, "You know, two wrongs don't make a

Old road from Langevin home to the Chase farm

right. Those boys will keep saying things if you argue and make them mad at you. Use your brain, Pat. And you can't be going to the teacher with every little problem you have with those boys. You have to get along with those kids. I'll say it again, the teacher's there to teach you to read and write."

After working for an hour or so, Dad suddenly looked up from his steady work, "Pat, it's time to quit. Let's call it a day. We've got other irons in the fire. I need to read the paper. You, too, have things to do."

"Okay!" To tell you the truth, grading potatoes was not my favorite chore. The smell of earth roamed around the basement as the dusty potatoes rattled along the rollers. The dust rolled up into the air. The potatoes were cold and that in turn cooled my hands uncomfortably.

Dad tidied up the grading machine and said, "Be sure to wash your hands. You know how much your mother dislikes dirt and dust. And fill the colander with a few potatoes. Mom says the kitchen bin is nearly empty."

I picked up the old colander with loose handles and filled it with potatoes. I started up the stairs. "That's done, Dad. That's one less thing to worry about."

In the kitchen, I dumped the potatoes into the old bin, set the colander on the floor near the basement's door, and found my way to the bathroom sink to wash my dusty hands.

The last time Gene was home he had told me that during World War II the U.S. government bought our potatoes to use for seed. "I was just a little kid, smaller than you are now. I remember that our potatoes were shipped to Long Island by train. The government hired farmers on the eastern part of Long Island to grow potatoes. When harvested, they were shipped to England to feed soldiers. That's why most farmers in Vermont grew potatoes. One farmer planted and harvested over one hundred fifty acres."

"Wow!" I exclaimed, "One hundred fifty acres! Am I glad we didn't live on that farm! How many potatoes is that anyway?"

"I don't know. But, during the war, Dad planted twice as many potatoes as he does now. The market was bet-

Flat farm fields often sported potatoes

ter then. One of my army buddies remembers the trains filled with potatoes passing by his home on Long Island when he was a little boy. He saw potatoes that maybe came from Dad's farm." Gene laughed.

Selling potatoes was important. We had so many, way too many for ourselves. Our seven acres created bins full to brimming. The need and desire for profits drove Dad's ambitions.

"So many farmers have stopped growing potatoes that now we have cornered the market around here. We have money to pay the property taxes." Dad chuckled as he sold bushel after bushel. During a conversation like that, all I could think about was that farmer and his one hundred fifty acres of potatoes!

Chapter 26

SAVING & SPENDING MONEY

*Money is like a sixth sense without which you cannot
make a complete use of the other five.*
William Somerset Maugham

For all of the jobs we kids worked at, we earned money.
Dad paid each of us $3 every month. During the busy
months of planting crops, the harvesting of potatoes,
squash, corn, and maple sugaring, we earned extra
money. We also earned more money by helping Mom
with her maple business at Christmastime.

Clarence worked fulltime on the farm now. He was
earning as much as an adult and, of course, he was
paid much more than the rest of us. He planned to own
the farm some day. He and Dad talked about forming a
partnership.

To encourage me to save my money when I turned six,
Dad and I visited the Randolph Savings Bank where I
opened a savings account. He had taken my brothers
and sisters there on or near their sixth birthday, too.

"A penny saved is a penny earned," Dad often declared. He warned us, "Now don't be penny wise and
pound foolish." Another of his favorites was, "Save your
pennies and the dollars will take care of themselves."

Every month on one of our trips to Randolph, we

walked into the bank with more money to deposit. We earned a tad more due to interest earnings.

"Here you are Patricia. Keep saving, and you'll have enough money for college," explained the teller. He showed me the new total in my account book. The little book fit into my pants pocket. I watched my savings account grow with interest.

Dad owned an old oak desk with a roll top. When the desk's top was rolled open, there in front of the writing area were rows of holes deep enough and wide enough to hold stacks of letters.

"Here's the place for your account book, right in this pigeon hole, along with your brothers' and sisters' books." Dad pointed to one small hole in the long rows. "You know that I lock the roll top when I'm not using my desk. Everything is safe in here." That was an odd statement. Dad locked his desk. Yet we had no locks on our inside or outside doors. The idea of anyone entering without knocking never gave us any worry.

My siblings and I saved a dollar for spending from our monthly allowance. Some of it was spent for books, comics, and other reading materials. We bought games such as dominoes, checkers, pick-up-sticks, bingo, jigsaw puzzles, and playing cards. We kids loved to play canasta. However, the lion's share of that dollar was spent on candy and movies.

"Can we go to the movies this weekend? Mom, can

244 HANDS IN THE EARTH

you drive us to the movies on Sunday night?" Raymond asked.

"You'll have to ask your father."

Raymond walked to the kitchen where Dad was reading the newspaper. "Hey, Dad can we go to the movies on Sunday night?"

"If it's all right with your mother. She's the one who has to drive you there."

The deed was done! We were going to the movies!

Movies cost twenty cents for kids and a little more for my older siblings. The candy sold at the theater was much more expensive than at Mr. Prescott's store.

"Those candy prices at the theater are ridiculous and just short of highway robbery. Only fools with nothing better to do with their money would spend it that way. Anyone who pays fifteen cents for a nickel candy bar is silly at best when the candy isn't worth a nickel to begin with. You all eat too much candy as it is," Dad complained.

Ray thought Dad should have been a preacher. "He'd be a good one the way he's always telling us what's best for us."

Raymond climbed on to his imaginary stage. With one arm raised, and with the other he used his index finger to point out his vision of Dad. Ray grimaced at just the right time, raised his voice, and with emphasis on certain words, he mimicked him.

"You kids eat too much candy. Well, who's the first to reach for the candy stashed in his desk? Just like a preacher, he doesn't practice what he says. And you should hear Dad when he sees a light on in a room with no one in it! He yells, who was the last person in here? Dad leaves his desk lamp on all the time! It burns night and day! He claims a stitch in time saves nine and then says don't put all of your eggs in one basket. Well, we don't have eggs to put into a basket and he doesn't know how to sew! So what does he know?"

We laughed along with Raymond. Gene had said, "Raymond, you're our actor in the making."

With Dad's lessons on frugality in mind when at the theater, we chose the warm, salty, and buttery popcorn. We each purchased our very own box for ten cents. A box of popcorn just for me was heaven on earth! I always hoped the contents of the box would last through the entire movie. That never happened. I gobbled up one popped kernel after another. Soon the box was empty and its contents gone. Vanished!

Mother drove us in our old Plymouth the five miles to the theater. Sometimes she came to the movies, but more often she'd say, as she dropped us off, "I'll be here when the movie ends. I'm going to visit Mrs. Bradbury," … or perhaps, "I am going to Mrs. Donahue's."

The theater owner knew that we were trustworthy. Dad taught us to be respectful of anyone who was an adult. The owner knew we wouldn't throw things around as some kids did. So some kids couldn't attend a movie without an adult.

"You need to use your brains not just your hands. You don't need someone watching over your every move. Be sensible. No one in this family needs a bad reputation. Be respectful of adults and their property. I want to be proud of you and behaving is one way to make me proud," Dad said.

Sometimes other kids threw popcorn and candy bar wrappers particularly when the movie was of no interest. The usher walked up and down the aisle, flashlight in hand shining it here and there, seldom able to locate the wrongdoers. During the ride home we talked about that.

"They're stupid to throw popcorn," I'd lecture to no one in particular. "It's such a waste and disturbs everybody. The usher shines her flashlight in my eyes and then I can't see the movie. Why are the bad kids in the theater if a grown up isn't with them?"

Raymond liked to get an argument going. He'd pipe up, "Well, that's nothing compared to you two little kids. It's no more foolish or stupid than covering your eyes because you're 'fraidy cats during the movie. You little kids embarrass me when you sit on the floor covering your ears with eyes closed too scared to watch the movie you've paid to see. What are you afraid of? Your own shadow?"

When we spoke at home about particularly scary movies like westerns, Alfred Hitchcock movies, or war stories, Dad wondered if a certain movie was worth seeing. *High Noon* and *The Gunfighter* were frightening westerns. *Rear Window*, a scary murder mystery directed by Alfred Hitchcock, gave me nightmares. *From Here to Eternity*, a World War II movie had parts that frightened me: fights, people going to jail, loud arguments, and other kinds of violence.

Ray was right. When the scene was too gruesome, noisy, or frightening, Sandy and I sat on the floor with closed eyes and ears covered just as Ray described.

We sat through silly movies like *Ma and Pa Kettle*. The Kettles were country bumpkins who made errors in judgment. Their children were noisy and messy. Everything the Kettles owned was falling apart, in a state of disrepair caused by neglect or age.

Dean Martin and Jerry Lewis movies were favorites. "I love Dean Martin. He's so handsome and snazzy, sensible, and serious. And I love to see him dance!" He was Sandy's idol.

Jerry Lewis played a bumbling dummy-type character. "He's silly and funny. I like him. I like the way he dances because he can't dance at all," I said.

"Pat, he can dance! It's all an act and he's really dancing." I wasn't convinced of Sandy's ideas about Jerry

Floyd's, formerly Prescott's, Store in Randolph Center

Lewis's dancing skills.

"Can those kinds of movies be worth the money you're spending? You're all poisoning your minds!" Dad observed. He returned to his newspaper, pencil and paper in hand. He wrote various numbers, worried over the news, and became absorbed in his figures and thoughts.

Newsreels were shown before the movie started. The reels showed news about the Korean War or the threat of Communism. A senator, named Joe McCarthy, was often shown arguing into the microphone about all the Communists in the government. He was scary. He reminded Sandy of a neighbor who was so deaf he shouted. He had forgotten that others could hear perfectly well, I guess.

We kids also spent our money on reading materials. We liked Roy Rogers and Dale Evans, Reggie, Archie, and Lucy comics. We traded our reading treasures. I traded my Lucy comics with my friend Christine. Harriet and Carolyn liked movie magazines and traded their Archie comics with friends.

On some Sunday evenings, we listened on the radio to the latest adventures of the Lone Ranger and his sidekick, Tonto. Harriet and Raymond couldn't miss "The Shadow Knows," a radio series with scary adventures.

The teachers particularly Miss Flanders, disapproved of movie magazines. Maybe she thought actors and the Hollywood lifestyle were not good role models for kids living in Vermont. If Miss Flanders found a movie magazine tucked in someone's desk, she took it.

During recess, Christine laughed, "I think Miss Flanders reads them."

"Really? Would she do that?" I asked.

Bernard added, "It's true. She reads them when we're all out here for recess. She puts all our papers to correct in front of her and then reads the movie magazine."

"How do you know that?" I asked.

"I've seen her when I had to stay in during recess to finish my workbook."

We bought and read the Hardy Boy series, Nancy Drew books, the Bobbsey Twins books, and others too.

We also spent our money on candy. We kids loved to go to Prescott's Store not far from our home. Mr. Prescott kept his gum, penny candies, and candy bars behind the counter. Trays of candies were lined up in cardboard boxes on wooden shelves.

Mom drove to the store almost every day to buy the *Boston Herald* for our dad. He liked to read the paper in the evening after all the day's work was done. We kids marched into Mr. Prescott's store, made our way behind the counter, and began the decision-making process of choosing our favorite candies.

"Mary, I know your children are honest. Let them go and select what they like." Mr. Prescott smiled.

I loved chewy peanut butter kisses and Mary Janes. These taffy-type candies were flavored with molasses and their centers oozed peanut butter. Each cost a penny. I loved Necco Wafers and Life Savers. A whole roll cost a nickel! Tootsie Roll Pops cost two cents. Tootsie Rolls and Double Bubble Bubblegum were favorite choices. Each cost a penny. Various flavored Kits were individually wrapped in packs of four, only a penny.

Actually there was no candy I didn't like. I loved Mars Bars, Mounds, Almond Joys, Three Musketeers, and Hershey bars with almonds. Each cost a nickel. Whatever my choice, my candy stash was used sparingly. I always wanted to have candy just in case.

"In case of what, Patty?" Sandy teased.

"You know, just in case."

Dad had his favorite candy, too. He kept a supply of Old Fashioned Creme Chocolates in his desk stored in a white paper bag. They were dome-shaped with tasty chocolate on the outside and pure creamy white vanilla flavored fondant on the inside. Dad was generous with his chocolates. He would hold out the little bag. "Here, have a candy," he'd say as he read over papers, letters, and bills piled high on his desk.

As soon as you'd pop one in your mouth, the chocolate and fondant melted right there on your tongue and soon the sweet taste was everywhere.

Aunt Almira said more times than I can count, "We had those candies when we were children. That's the only kind of candy your father wanted. He had a sweet tooth and he still has it. I can tell."

Old Fashioned Cremes were kept in a large glass case with many other bulk candies at Belmain's Department Store. You could buy just a few, a whole pound, or more.

As for Aunt Almira, she too had a sweet tooth. She liked Necco's pink Canada Wintergreen Mints and the white Canada Mints with a strong peppermint flavor. She shared her candy.

Sandy charmed and coaxed our aunt into giving her many treats. "Auntie," she'd say snuggling up close to her, "you have the best candy. I love those pink ones.

Do you have any left, Auntie?"

"Come with me, dear." Aunt Almira smiled, carefully put aside her crocheting, heaved herself up from her easy chair, and taking Sandy's hand, they walked to her bedroom. She opened that special bureau drawer, removed that magic bag and held it out to Sandy. "Here you are, Sandy. Take a few."

Sandy, delighted as always, reached into the small white bag, gathered a fistful of the fresh pink candies in her little hand, smiled like a wily fox, and scampered off, mission accomplished. "Thanks, Auntie!" Sandy's expression of delight and gratitude resounded throughout the entire house.

Now that winter had set in, we had more idle time for our favorite activities. Yet, we were up early every day to do chores, and again after school we'd complete the necessary activities to keep our animals cared for and happy.

Chapter 27

FEEDING OUR ANIMALS

Come, father and mother and sister and brother,
Come, all of you, turn to and help one another.
Edgar Guest

When the cows were outside during an infrequent warm winter day, they danced and pranced around. They shook their heads and frolicked about.

"They're letting off steam," Dad chuckled. "They like the sun."

Our animals needed to be fed twice a day, every day. Cows ate grain, summer and winter. During the hot summer months they ate grass outside in the pasture. They drank water from the stream that meandered through the pastures or from the barnyard watering tub.

In the wintertime, hay stored in the barn was added to the cows' diet. Dark, thick molasses was poured over the hay. During this time of year the cows lived in the barn. They lumbered out to the barnyard for exercise, but not for too long because of the cold weather.

Dad and Clarence kept records of the amount of milk each cow produced and that determined the amount of grain each cow was fed. Clarence used a scale to weigh the milk. He wrote the amount on special charts.

Dad told me, "The best milkers get two scoops of grain.

The others get just one scoop."

The cows loved the grain and licked up the last bits with outstretched velvety tongues. They looked at us with big, round eyes, and if they could speak, they'd bellow, "Hey, give us more of that tasty stuff."

I fed warm milk to the calves just given up by the cows. They ate hay and grain, too. As I fed them, I petted each one. When I fed my 4-H calf, Suzie, I held a little grain in my outstretched hand. Her muzzle and tongue licked the grain from my hand.

"Try that," I urged Sandy to hold out her hand.

"Oh, Patty, that tickles! Their tongues are so soft! And wet! Yuck!"

When the calves were a little older, they no longer drank their mother's milk. Now they drank water and ate more grain and hay as they grew. My sisters and I carried the hay bales from the haymow that had been stacked there so carefully last summer. We broke open each bale using a knife to cut the twine that had held it together. We fluffed up the condensed forage.

Sometimes, the hay reminded me of the warm sunny summer when the fresh hay bales had smelled so pungent. My friend Christine always said, "Our dog Tippy smells like fresh mown hay."

During the winter, Dad added dark molasses to the hay. Once the hay bales had been opened, fluffed up, and placed in the mangers, Clarence or my father spread the thick molasses, thinned a little with warm water, over the hay using a large dipper and a pail.

"This molasses contains nutrients important for our cows' health. In fact, some people use molasses for medicinal purposes because it contains iron and people need iron, too," Dad said.

Molasses is what remains after the sugar crystals have been removed by boiling sugar cane stalks. Sometimes the canes are boiled twice, even three times, to get more of the sugar to crystallize. The molasses gets darker and stronger every time the cane is boiled.

Our cows ate the molasses-covered hay with almost as much enthusiasm as the little pigs going to their trough for food. The cows used their long tongues to slurp stray droplets into their mouths.

Dad bought molasses, almost black in color, in barrels at Dustin's feed store. He or Clarence traveled to the feed store with the truck and refilled the barrels. The molasses was thick like soft fudge, so thick it moved slowly. It was, well, as slow as molasses running up hill.

"You're as slow as molasses! Stop dragging your feet," Dad sometimes admonished us. We never wanted to hear that!

The pigs and the piglets ate a variety of foods: the potato peelings, apple cores, peapods, cornhusks, corncobs, and other kitchen waste. Their four feet moved like a car out of control on slippery ice when going after food. "They think they haven't eaten food for days," Dad laughed.

The Yorkshires especially favored their daily mash, a grain mixed with warm water. The little ones squealed loudly and ran up to their trough traveling so fast they sped right into it as each competed for the best position. Their curly little tails always rotated like a whirlybird. They showed no manners at all!

"Your muffin mixture looks like the mash we feed the pigs." Sandy liked to tease Raymond.

"Well! Look whose finding fault with my cooking. Is that Sandy, a little kid, who doesn't know how to boil water? You know, Sandy, talk is cheap!" Raymond pointed a finger at Sandy, a wry smile on his face.

The pigs lived in a big pen at one end of the barn. A large tub held their water. Their long, narrow trough held the mash and other food. Their pen was covered with straw, that is, when they hadn't eaten it. If I walked up to the pen with food, well, what an amusing show they performed.

However, if I walked by the pigpen to go to the haymow to see the mousers, they met me with a disdainful non-caring look. Only their snouts quivered as each sniffed out a possible food source.

"Pigs can smell food a mile away. If you don't have food for them, they could care less about what you're up to," Dad explained.

Our piglets were sold to people who had no barns so we cared for them until they were grown. Or buyers stopped

Interior of dairy barn, 1950s style

by and selected one to take to their sheds. The piglets when large and porky were then slaughtered for food. If you have eaten pork chops, pork roast, bacon, ham, or sausage then you have benefited from a pig's life on earth.

Food was provided for our family in the same way. It bothered me to think about that. The little piglets were cute, not quite cuddly, but cute for sure. The two or three piglets that remained with us were friendly, with a personality that seemed to say, "Oh! Look at me! Do you notice how handsome I am becoming? Take a look at me!"

Carolyn decided at an early age to eat no meat. She liked our Black Angus calf aptly named Blackie. She often offered Blackie apples or a little grain from her hand.

Whiting Milk Company at Randolph train station

She was disturbed when two years later he appeared on our table as food.

It bothered Carolyn to think back on Blackie's life. He was a steer, a gentle, friendly soul, and loved spending time outside in the green pastures during the summer. He loved apples from our old orchard, the summer squash grown too big for human consumption, the pea pods, and corn husks. Blackie liked being stroked under his neck and held his head high when we visited and petted him.

We were learning, however, that most farm animals could not be adopted as pets. "Animals serve many purposes and one purpose is to provide food. Have you heard about the food chain?" Dad taught us about the need for meat and other foods.

Chapter 28

TREACHEROUS TOOLS

An ounce of prevention is worth a pound of cure.
A Proverb

Late one cold winter day, Clarence had begun the milking by himself. Dad was grading potatoes. The rest of us kids began feeding the cows and calves. Sandy and I brought hay bales from the haymow. Carolyn scooped grain from the cart, and fed each cow as she pushed the cart along the long aisle in front of their manger. With our hands, Sandy and I began fluffing up the hay that had been released from its twine. Harriet was carrying hay with a pitchfork to the calves.

Raymond worked with us this time. He digressed from his task. More to the point, let's say he was off track. Clarence reminded him, "Raymond get the hot water and mix it with the molasses. And pour it over the cows' hay."

"Okay," Raymond answered, "just as soon as I finish helping Harriet pitch hay to the calves."

Carolyn said, "Ray, I don't have enough grain to feed all the cows."

Raymond pushed the wheelbarrow to the stacks in the storage area. He loaded two sacks of grain.

"Here's your grain, Carolyn, delivered with the speed of lightning on this cold, wintry afternoon. Your servant at your ..." Raymond suddenly howled. He shrieked as he fell to the floor in front of the haymow. The wheelbarrow skidded to a stop.

A pitchfork had gone through his shoe and foot exposing one tine through the front part of his shoe right in between his big toe and sole of his foot. Sandy and I winced in horror and stared in shock. Carolyn came running when she heard his screams. Clarence and Harriet, too.

"Oh, it hurts," he moaned. "It hurts. Somebody get Mother to help me." Tears filled his eyes.

Blood trickled up through the top of his foot and oozed out the bottom of his shoe as he lay there. The hay surrounding his foot soaked up red blood. He was as pale as a ghost. Harriet cradled his head in her hands.

"Can you get up?" I asked.

"Stupid, how can I get up with this pitchfork in my foot? Get Mom! Somebody get Mother to help me."

Clarence turned to Carolyn, "Go get Mom!" She was well on her way, her senses about her, to the house in a race against time. Sandy followed closely behind. Mom had had some nurse's training before she married Dad. She seldom came to the barn, but this time she hurried into the barn with my sisters.

Clarence soothed Ray as best he could and asked,

"Do you need a drink of water? What can I do for you? Ray?"

Ray trembled as a leaf in an autumn storm. He mumbled incoherently.

Although it seemed forever, Mom arrived and took a look at Ray, worry on her face, "Oh, Raymond, what has happened? This will hurt some. Now, don't move." Without waiting for a response, she leaned over and with a mighty yank removed the pitchfork. Blood spurted from his shoe. Raymond was in agony. Tears rolled down his cheeks. Harriet sat on the floor beside him.

"I'll put the pitchfork on its hook before somebody else steps on it," Clarence grabbed the pitchfork from Mom's hand.

"Oh it hurts, Mama. It hurts so bad."

"I know, son. Harriet, run to the house and get clean towels. Dad is coming with the car and he's already called the hospital. I'll wrap your foot. But first, let me remove your shoe. This may hurt a little. Stay very still. Now don't move your foot."

Raymond moaned as Mom quickly untied his shoe and pulled at it. He turned whiter, groaned, and gasped in pain. Mother wiped away his tears with her handkerchief. "Now be still," Mom said. "How did this happen, Raymond? What were you doing?"

"I was using the wheelbarrow and ..."

Harriet interrupted, raced into the barn. "Dad is backing the car closer to the barn. Here are the clean towels, Mom."

"I'll wrap them around Raymond's foot." Mom reached for the towels.

"Raymee, does it hurt a lot? I'm so sorry you hurt your foot," Sandy stammered.

"You have to stand up, Raymond. Lean on me. Don't stand on your injured foot. Lean on me, okay?" Mom was patient.

"No, Mom, let me." Raymond was quiet as his brother put an arm around his hunched shoulders and the other around his legs and picked him up. Our giant lifted Ray as if he were a baby. Ray managed to stand on his good leg. He gingerly held his injured foot off the floor in front of him as Clarence steadied him. The towels were soaking up blood.

"It hurts, Mom." Raymond used his little boy voice.

"I know. I know. You'll be all right. I'm taking you to the hospital as soon as he backs the car closer."

Dad appeared. "What has happened? I'll help Raymond. What has happened?" he repeated.

"I stepped on the pitchfork when I was wheeling in oats for Carolyn. She didn't have enough grain for the whole herd. So, I pitched in to help her, and ...."

Clarence lifted Raymond and carried him outside as easily as a baby. Dad followed and quickly opened the car's door.

"Call Dr. Woodruff's office. Tell whoever answers that we need some help, a stretcher or something," Mom yelled back as she hopped into the car and raced away.

"Right after I call the doctor's office, I'll come back and help you finish the milking, Clarence. The potatoes can wait. You girls finish feeding and watering the cows and calves. Don't forget to feed the pigs their mash."

"I hope Raymee will be okay," Sandy cried.

"Me, too," I mumbled.

"The doctor will know what to do. He'll be fine," Dad comforted a sobbing Sandy. "Sandy, Raymond's in good hands. Dr. Woodruff will take care of him. I'll be right back. I've got to call the hospital again." Dad hurried to the house.

Sandy seemed doubtful and remained quiet for the rest of chore time. No one had much to say. When all the chores were finished, everyone returned home, ate supper, and waited for Mom and Raymond's return from the hospital.

***

Finally, we heard the car in the driveway. Raymond, with Mom at his side, struggled into the house with crutches. His bandaged foot dangled in front of him, slightly bent, to keep from making contact with the floor. He sat on the sofa and set his crutches beside it. Harriet brought him food we had saved for him. He ate little, drank a glass of milk, and surveyed his family who all waited for news of his well-being. Some of his paleness had diminished and he seemed in less pain.

Mom asked, "Can you little kids get the packages from the car? Be careful not to drop anything. Take the flashlight."

"Okay," Sandy said. I picked up the flashlight. In the backseat, Sandy and I found great packages of bandages, one bottle filled with pills, and another with antiseptic. A paper listed many of the things Dr. Woodruff directed Raymond to do. Another bag held blood-soaked towels and Raymond's bloody sock. We returned to the living room and handed everything to Mom.

"Can you take these bloody towels to the washroom, Pat?" Mom asked.

"Raymond's bloody sock is in this sack, too," I said.

Raymond began telling us about what he called "my great adventure."

"First, Dr. Woodruff asked me how I stepped on a pitchfork. He asked, doesn't the pitchfork have a safe storage place? Then he said lay down here on that examining table. I'll help you. He supported my legs while I moved over from the gurney on to his examining table using my elbows."

"He removed the towels wrapped around my foot. It hurt when he took off my blood-soaked sock because by now the blood had dried to my foot like glue to paper. I held back my tears. I didn't want to seem like a sissy.

He looked this way and that way all around my foot. I thought at first he didn't know what to do. Is Dr. Woodruff confused?"

Although Raymond laughed, the rest of us heard his story in stony silence for we were aware of the dangers of open wounds and infections that can attack an immune system in the human body. Around barns and animals there are many germs that could enter your body through your blood.

Dad answered, "Raymond, Dr. Woodruff would know what to do. He's Randolph's best doctor."

Ray continued, "Dr. Woodruff turned, washed his hands, put on his rubber gloves, and asked the nurse for hot, soapy water. She quickly brought him a basin. Dr. Woodruff opened a bottle and dumped some foul-smelling antiseptic into the hot water. He and the nurse washed my foot. He said, "Just in case your tetanus shot has worn out, I'm giving you another tetanus shot."

"Some gift," laughed Ray as he babied his arm. Raymond was an impressive storyteller. He winced at just the right times, showed agony when appropriate, and imitated Dr. Woodruff's voice perfectly. From the sofa, he was on stage.

Still, my family remained quiet and serious. Antiseptic and a tetanus shot meant that Dr. Woodruff was worried about an infection or blood contamination in Raymond's body just as the doctor had been with Harriet last summer. I noticed that Harriet was as white as a sheet and seemed dazed.

"Dr. Woodruff gave me a pain pill and handed a bottle of pills to Mom. He said you must stay off your foot and you must remove the bandages every day, wash your foot, and coat the wound with this special antiseptic. You have a serious injury. You've bruised a couple of small bones in your foot. A barn has numerous germs and bacteria. Keep your wound clean and wrapped in bandages to prevent any infection. Raymond, you're old enough to do this yourself. Your mother is very busy and has enough to do without taking care of you. Can you do this?"

"Oh, yes, I can, I told Dr. Woodruff." Raymond grinned with pride as he told the story.

"The nurse left the room for a moment, returned, and handed me these crutches. She said be sure not to put any weight on your foot. She pointed at it just as if I wouldn't know which foot got skewered. "

She told me, "As your injury heals, it must not be disturbed. Don't go to the barn until your foot has healed completely."

Raymond finished by saying, "I'm glad about orders to stay away from that dirty, old nasty barn! Lucky me!" He looked around the room at our solemn faces. "I'll do everything Dr. Woodruff tells me to do. I'll live through this. Don't worry."

Ray used the crutches and hopped around the house. "I can't get up and down the stairs very well with crutches. I'll sleep on the sofa."

When Ray returned to high school, he wore several socks to warm his foot. He called the Bigelows and asked for time off due to his injury with the devil's pitchfork. He kept his balance with the crutches and hopped around easily after a few days of practice.

"Is this the Easter bunny a little early this year?" one friend at school asked.

"Yes, it is, and where are my carrots, Brenda? My Easter basket is empty," Raymond kidded.

Raymond got used to crutches and hurried around the kitchen as he continued his baking duties. He sometimes maneuvered on one crutch. Good naturedly, he said, "Everybody around here gets hungry whether or not I can walk."

He made a game of hopping up and down the stairs using the banister to guide him after he announced, "My foot is getting better. I can go back to my room and finally get a good night's sleep."

"Be careful, Raymond. Don't put any weight on that foot yet," Mom advised.

"All right, Nurse Mary."

Soon his foot healed and the crutches were returned to the hospital. Raymond had scars that looked like red

Dr. Woodruff, Randolph's noted doctor

buttons, one on his foot's top and the other on the bottom. He returned to his job with Mrs. Bigelow.

"Finally, I can walk normally again. I was having a heck of a time carrying my books, my trumpet, and maneuvering around with those old crutches." Ray sounded happy to have his life back to normal.

***

"Our family knows that our tools are dangerous and require caution. Every tool has a place for safe storage, Raymond. Think about Clarence's toolbox," Dad said during supper one night.

"Clarence gets upset if we forget to return something to

his toolbox. Forget to return his little saw, wow, the roof falls in until it's back in the box!" Raymond laughed.

Clarence shot back, "Well, everything does cost money! Leave something here or there and then it gets wet, rusty, or lost and then can't be used."

Dad continued, "The larger tools like our axes, saws, and hoes have their places. Even the pitchforks belong on special hooks."

"I know, Dad," Raymond said quietly.

"A stitch in time saves nine. Think of the stitches this carelessness brought you, son. An ounce of prevention is worth a pound of cure."

"I know Dad. There's a place for everything and everything in its place," Raymond said nervously.

With a solemn face, Dad searched Raymond's face. Everyone was quiet.

"I've learned that, for sure," Ray added.

Chapter 29

FROM SAP TO SYRUP

*Life is full and overflowing with the new. But it is necessary
to empty out the old to make room for the new to enter.*
Eileen Caddy

One evening in mid-February, I sat at the table completing my schoolwork. Sandy was practicing her times tables with little cards. Dad and Clarence were there at the table, too.

"Tomorrow, let's get the sap buckets out of storage and begin tapping the trees, Clarence. I feel spring in the air."

"Right, Dad. The snow isn't too deep this year, and I can quickly clear a path through the woodlot road with the tractor and plow. One swing through the woods should clear it enough to get our tapping gear in there. Have you called Mr. Kibby and talked with Bernie?"

"Oh, yes. They both agree that we can tap their maples again this year."

I'll swing by Mr. Kibby's woodlot right after I clear ours. Like I said, it shouldn't take long."

Our family set out about eight hundred buckets in our maple orchard and on the maples along the surrounding roads.

"Can I help you after school tomorrow, Daddy?" Sandy

asked.

"Yes, Clarence and I can use your help."

"I'll help too," I said. "Bobby hasn't been in school all week. He's helping his dad with their trees. He'll miss the Valentine's party."

"He will? Will he get your Valentine card?" Sandy asked.

"Yes, we made folders for our Valentines and Miss Flanders made one for him. His cards are all in there. They will be waiting for him when he gets back after school vacation."

The maple sugaring season had begun. That meant that every day after school, during winter vacation, and right up through spring vacation in April, our whole family would be busy producing maple syrup. In fact, Miss Flanders said to us, "School vacations are planned with farm chores in mind."

That next day, Dad got out all the sap buckets, covers, and spouts and loaded them onto the wagon. He uncovered the gathering tank from its year-long rest and cleaned it.

Clarence plowed open the roads. When he returned Dad said, "I'm ready when you are, son."

"All I need from my toolbox is the hammer and hand drill."

When the tapping began, Clarence quickly drilled holes about two inches into the maple tree trunks and hammered in the spouts. The holes were about the diameter of a pencil. The hollow metal spouts allowed the watery sweet-tasting sap to escape from the tree and fill each bucket. "Think of the spout as a tiny funnel," Dad had explained to Sandy and me when we were really little.

Some trees were large enough to have four or five taps. Smaller trees might have one or two taps. Dad carried buckets and covers and placed a bucket on each of the spout's little hook. Then he covered the bucket with a special lid to keep out snow, sleet, and debris.

When we returned from school, Sandy rushed to change her clothes. "Come on, Pat, let's hurry so we can help. Daddy told me that Harriet and Carolyn will feed the animals today."

"Do you see the little hook on each spout? Do you see the hole at the bucket's rim?" Dad showed us what to do.

"Oh, yeah, Daddy, I remember from last year."

"Pat, you slide the covers onto each bucket. Dad and I have been doing this all afternoon." Clarence reminded me how a cover slid over the top of the bucket and attached to the bucket's rim.

Dad returned home to prepare for the milking and to help Carolyn and Harriet with their chores.

"Clarence takes such big steps in the snow, Patty. We have to make our own path."

Hollyhock Lodge where Raymond worked during high school

For him, the snow wasn't so deep because he and Dad were both so big. For us little kids it was a struggle to maneuver up a snow bank and down its other side.

Within a few days, all of the trees were tapped. Now Dad waited for the perfect weather. Just as during the haying season, the weather reports were listened to carefully. The sap "ran" during certain weather conditions. Those conditions were cold nights below freezing, and warm days above freezing. When ideal, the liquid dripped continuously through the spouts into each bucket, drop by drop. We knew that it takes almost forty gallons of sap to make one gallon of syrup.

"We're in the middle of a run. We'll collect the sap today. It's a good thing you girls are on vacation this week," Dad said. Pail after pail of sap was collected and dumped into the gathering tank as the tractor pulled it through the woodlot. The tank sat on a sledge-type wagon with inflated rubber tires instead of sled runners.

"The tank is full, Dad. I'll make a run to the sugarhouse." Clarence drove toward the sugarhouse to deposit the sap into a larger holding tank.

Sandy and I rode along. We were strong enough to lift a half pail of sap at a time and now we had a chance to ride and rest.

"Did Johnny give you a Valentine card, Sandy?"

"Oh, yes, and he gave me little heart-shaped candies that said 'Be Mine' and 'Wow!' "

"What about Bobby? What did he give you?"

"Remember, he missed school all week because he's helping his dad with their trees. He'll be back after the vacation, I think."

"Oh, yeah," I forgot.

We saw a lot of Uncle Jim during this time of year for it was he who was in control of syrup production, his hobby and his job. After his mail route was finished for the day, he drove to the sugarhouse in his truck. He opened the faucet on the holding tank that allowed the sap to flow into the evaporator. He fired up the furnace using the wood we had stored there last summer.

Soon billowy steam caused by the heated and evaporating sap filled the sugarhouse and wafted out of doors through the ventilation system in the roof.

Uncle Jim tended the hot fire until the sap had condensed to syrup. He added more sap to one part of the evaporator as the boiling liquid began its journey toward maple syrup into another part of the big evaporator. He determined its consistency as the sap boiled, by watching the syrup fall from a shovel-like ladle held in his hand high over the steamy evaporator.

"Why do you do that?" I had asked him when I was really little.

"The syrup needs to be just right. I fill this ladle with the sticky stuff and if it sheets or spreads when I let it flow from the ladle then I know it is almost syrup."

"Oh, it looks like syrup, but sometimes you say it isn't ready yet."

"I use that as an estimate, Pat. Now, I'll put some syrup into this cylindrical container. Watch. I put a hydrometer into it and I take a reading on its gauge. That tells me the density of the syrup. Every liquid has its own density, even syrup. When the syrup reaches its correct density, I must pour the syrup off the evaporator quickly. I use this faucet. The hot syrup - don't get too close, Pat-flows through a felt strainer and into this ten-gallon can. The strainer removes minerals and niter that is mixed with the syrup."

"Uncle Jim, you're good at explaining things." He messed up my hair just like Dad.

Maple taps (note the high snowbanks)

He showed me how to take the temperature of the syrup. He used a thermometer and it read 219 degrees. "This is another way to know the syrup is ready," explained Uncle Jim.

Samples of our syrup were compared to small bottles that ran from light to dark in color. The samples were certified by the Vermont Maple Sugar Association and approved by the State of Vermont. The lighter it was in color the better the quality.

Fancy grade was the best. "Look at your pancakes this

morning. The syrup sparkles on them." Dad was proud of his Fancy grade syrup.

Grade A followed closely behind and following that was another Grade A amber, slightly darker in color. "Most people don't notice the difference between the two. The only difference I notice is in the color. Raymond, your maple desserts are best flavored with Grade A. You could sell your cookies and pies at Mr. Prescott's store. Mary, your maple-flavored ham could be sold there, too," Dad bragged.

"Mom, your baked beans are so good. They have a strong taste of maple in them." Raymond loved anything with maple flavor.

"Anyone who bakes beans uses Grade B. That has the best flavor for them," Mom answered.

A Grade C, lowest in value, was produced at the end of the season. It was dark in color, almost the color of the molasses we spread on the cows' hay. Dad sold Grade C syrup to companies that manufactured maple products. Natural medicines, maple extract, and some foods were flavored with this low grade C syrup. Those products could not be sold as 100 percent maple. But, the products' maple flavor was authentic.

"Grade C is to syrup what crumbs are to bread," Dad said. "It's worth so little we probably shouldn't even bother to boil so late in the season."

Late in the day, the syrup was brought to our house in

Uncle Jim's truck. But if Uncle Jim had to work far into the evening, mother packed him a basket.

"Can you little kids deliver this basket to Uncle Jim? Hold the basket steady so nothing spills or gets mixed up."

"Yes, we'll go, Mom." Sandy and I delighted in delivering his food. We were careful to hold the basket with its contents steady as we hurried down the hill, past the little pond, and turned on to the lane where at its end the sugarhouse sat tucked up against the edge of the sugar bush.

"Hi, there, girls. Do you have something for me? Gosh am I ever hungry! You're just in time." Uncle Jim rubbed his tummy, a smile on his face.

"Mom cooked you some supper." We handed him our carrier. Carefully, he uncovered the big towel that kept his food warm.

"Oh, your mother sent me some pot roast with mashed potatoes and gravy! Corn and peas, too, is that what I see? And look at this! A hearty slice of your mother's homemade bread with butter? No! Two slices here! And a thermos of hot, fresh coffee? I'm a lucky guy. A home-cooked meal! You both thank your mother for me."

Uncle Jim, tall and lanky, removed his newspaper and magazines from the ancient rocking chair and sat on the only furniture in the sugarhouse and enjoyed his dinner.

Maple syrup cans picturing old-fashioned way of sugaring

Clarence had said, "That chair is dilapidated, Uncle Jim. You should use it for firewood. We'll get you another."

"Why burn it, Clarence? It's the most comfortable furniture in here."

Sandy and I grinned at the way Uncle Jim loved what he called "home cooking." Sandy waited impatiently as he dug in, forkful after forkful of home-cooked food. She could wait no longer. "Darn it. We forgot your dessert."

"Why that's okay, Sandy, I have enough here. If I need something sweet, I'll have a tad of maple syrup. Now don't fret."

Impulsively, breaking into laughter, Sandy held out one hand that exposed a carefully wrapped slice of Ray-

Samples for grading maple syrup

mond's pie of the day. Uncle Jim's eyes danced.

"You're joking with me, are you, Sandy? You're a good-humored child. Am I right, Patty?"

"Sandy always has something funny to say."

Sandy began her dance, twisting this way and that. Uncle Jim and I laughed with my little sister.

Soon we were on our way home. As darkness approached, we passed the peepers in the pond. We weren't quiet so they were warned and still until any danger passed. The chorus resumed as we climbed and reached the top of the hill where our house sat.

Uncle Jim and Dad were friends. They had been neighbors many years ago when they were both bachelors. He was Harriet and Gene's godfather. He remembered all of us on our birthdays with a two-dollar bill. We loved him as if he were kin.

Uncle Jim worked as a rural mail carrier for the United States Postal Service. Because he was our friend, and because his mail route was at the halfway point when he arrived at our house, he was ready for a break. Up early, he had sorted the mail, bundled it, delivered it to homes, and driven his truck over many bumpy dirt roads.

If he was late, he blamed it on the condition of the roads. Snow or snowdrifts, muddy roads in the springtime, cows crossing during the summer, and the leaf peepers in autumn were all reasons for arriving late. People knew Uncle Jim traveled over Randolph's most poorly kept dirt and gravel roads.

"If the mail gets through today," Dad said, "then it's because Jim is at the wheel. No one else can get out of their driveway because of this storm!"

One of the few people Lassie never barked at was Uncle Jim. Instead she ran up to him, tail wagging, and as patiently as a dog can, wiggled, and waited for a dog's favorite greeting. Uncle Jim ignored the mandatory mailbox, walked into our kitchen, handed the mail to my mother, and sat down at the table.

"Good morning, Mary, Raymond. Hi, kids. How are all of you today?"

"We're all fine," answered Mom. A chorus of "Hi, Uncle

Jim!" resounded around the room.

"That's good coffee, Mary."

"I just brewed a fresh pot as always. I'm glad you like my coffee, Jim. Raymond always likes it."

Dad and Uncle Jim talked about many things. In early spring, the sugarhouse was a high priority. Now their conversation turned to sugaring, the sap runs, the weather's influence, the operation of the evaporator, the furnace in the sugarhouse, and the wood supply for the firebox. Dad had said, "The price for maple syrup has gone up this year. I never thought we'd sell what we made last year, but the cans have disappeared from the shelves, haven't they?"

The syrup was canned and sold in various sized containers from pints to gallons. Dad used a ladle and funnel to fill each one. Of course, our family consumed maple products. We enjoyed sweetening our cereal with maple syrup. We poured syrup over ice cream. It sweetened many desserts. Maple syrup was used for Mom's candy and maple spread business. She was busiest during the Christmas season.

The cans were decorated with drawings of handsome horses pulling a sledge with a wooden tank, the old way sap was collected and brought to the sugarhouse. Dad had phased out the old and plain, shiny cans. A label for each grade of syrup was placed at the top of the can. On one side of the can, a label indicated that the syrup was from our maple business.

Raymond E. Chase Farm
Pure Vermont Maple Syrup
Randolph Center, Vermont

At the end of the sugaring season, we kids helped remove the buckets and lids from the trees. Clarence pulled the spouts out with the hammer's claws. The spouts were washed and rinsed, all eight hundred, in hot, soapy water. The galvanized buckets and their lids were washed too, rinsed, and stacked to dry in the sun. When dry, they were stacked one inside the other and stored in the backroom shed and waited for another season.

Because my mother used butternuts in her maple fudge, during autumn we gathered up butternuts from our trees and stayed ahead of the squirrels that coveted them. We filled baskets and burlap bags full to the brim.

The butternut shell was so hard that Dad used a hammer to break them open. "A butternut is a hard nut to crack!" Dad joked. "Mary, we'll have to buy extra butternuts next year. Your mail-order business is growing."

We also cut slab wood during the summer to fuel the firebox. Clarence drove to the mill and loaded our truck with the waste wood, the bark from cut logs. Then it was cut into manageable lengths with a special circular saw powered by the tractor. We stacked the wood in the shed at the sugarhouse.

"That slab wood is so cheap the mill owner might as well give it away," Dad laughed.

Old cedar fence posts, worn-out wooden baskets, boxes, and cardboard were burned in the firebox. We used cut-up stumps and roots from our land-clearing project for firewood.

You may be wondering why the maple sugaring season is called that and not the maple syrup season, or perhaps the sap season. And you may wonder why the sugarhouse is not referred to as the syrup house. Native Americans boiled sap until it granulated and became solid. Early American settlers also boiled the sap until it became a sugary solid. They called their product maple sugar. Because there was a shortage of containers for liquids, saving a large cake of sugar was easy. Only one large wooden tub or perhaps a large earthenware container could hold the sugary mass.

Mr. Cooley told Clarence, "I remember as a boy, I loved maple sugar. When Mom sent me to the pantry to get some, I'd cut off a sugary piece, and pop it into my mouth. Then I'd cut off a large chunk for Mom, place it in a pot with a tad of water, and heat it until the sugary mass returned to a liquid. We'd have instant maple syrup!"

When all the work had been completed, Dad drove over to Mr. Kibby's house and then to Mr. Langevin's farm. "This gallon of syrup is for allowing me to use your trees, Mr. Kibby. Thank you." And to Bernie, he said, "*Voila!* [There it is!] One hand washes the other, Bernie. *Merci.*"

Chapter 30

MOTHER'S MAPLE BUSINESS

I slept and dreamed that life was beauty.
I woke - and found that life was duty.
Ellen Sturgis Hooper

"Carolyn and Harriet, can you take the rubber molds out of the pantry? I need both sizes," Mom asked one evening.

"We'll wash them, too," Harriet answered. "They'll be ready for your maple sugar cakes."

The rubber molds were used to shape maple sugar cakes into maple leaves. Mom also processed pure maple spread and maple butternut fudge. She added only syrup and butternuts to her candies.

When school let out the next day, two weeks or so before Christmas, we donned our winter scarves, coats, mittens, boots, and hats and raced out the school door toward home. A super, sweet job awaited us. Harriet had returned from school on the high school bus and was already at work with Mom. Raymond was at work with Mrs. Bigelow.

On my way home on those cold winter days, I thought about the sugaring season that coincided with warm spring days and the sounds of water trickling along the roadsides with ever decreasing snow banks. Mud prevailed as Vermont began its fifth season.

Now, however, the landscape seemed painted, stationary, locked in place and time, covered with snow and ice. Strong winds would whip up the snow, and the few leaves remaining on the maples and oaks rustled. The pines would shake and snowstorms would follow. When over, everything settled into stillness.

"Look out for icy spots, Sandy. Now don't slip and fall," I kidded her with Dad's advice.

"Be careful! This family doesn't need any more broken bones," Sandy kidded right back.

Soon we bounded into our kitchen. The table was covered with trays of fudge, large and small maple sugar leaves, and one pound tins of maple spread. The aroma hit our senses first. Our eyes danced and our taste buds yearned for what lay before us. My sisters and I stared at the kitchen table laden with trays of maple products waiting to be weighed, packed, labeled, and shipped.

Mom greeted each of us, "Wash your hands with soap. Then we'll get to work filling these orders." Quickly, we removed our mittens and other winter clothing. We lined up at the bathroom sink to carefully wash our hands. We were ready to work!

Mom prepared maple products using our syrup and Christmastime was her busiest season. She sold her sweets to many customers nearby and to people in far off Massachusetts.

"Mary, your candies are as sweet and pure as the morning sun," Dad had bragged.

Mom took pride in her products. "I don't know anyone who is without a sweet tooth," she teased.

Each of Mom's maple products was heated to just the right temperature. She used our electric stove and a large kettle. The maple leaves needed to be soft, fondant-like on the inside, yet with enough of a shell-like consistency on the outside to hold the leaf-shape when released from the molds. The butternut fudge, too, had a fondant-like consistency, creamy and smooth. Butternuts added a nutty crunch to every bite.

The maple spread could be easily spread with a knife over toast, pancakes, or waffles. "Most people who order maple spread use it as icing on cakes, cupcakes, and cookies," Mom had told us.

People stopped by our house in their cars to pick up ready-made products. At this time of year, just prior to the holidays, Dad drove to the post office several times to ship packages to people who lived out of town. Many of our customers lived in Massachusetts. Dad's cousin Cass and her husband lived near Boston.

Dad bragged, "Cousins Cass and Herb are good with sales for this family, Mary. She even has her doctor buying our products and he's a good customer. He pays right away and he orders plenty of syrup, too. Postage is so high we have to raise our prices. Next year, Mary, we'll notify our customers that the prices have increased. The packing boxes cost more now. When our supply is used up, we'll be spending more for replacements. The work you're doing is worth a raise, too."

"We can use more money for holiday expenses. We need things for the house." How much higher the prices were going to be had not been determined, but Mom agreed with Dad.

"Let's put these candy boxes together first. Sandy, you're good at that. Pat can help you, too."

"Oh, goody, Mom, I love that job. That's so easy." Sandy started the task right away.

"How do you put them together so fast, Sandy? For every one I've put together, you've done two or three."

"It's easy! It's so easy, just like making paper airplanes."

"What do you know about making paper airplanes?"

"That's for me to know and for you to find out!" Sandy coyly answered.

The little boxes had been purchased flat. We shaped them by folding and interlocking the bottom connectors until they formed a little box. The cover contained a flap that folded into the box after the candies and the waxed papers were placed inside.

Meanwhile, Mom used the large milk pitcher to carefully pour and fill each leaf-shaped mold with hot, maple sweets. Her supply was growing.

"Carolyn, can you help Harriet remove the leaves from the molds?" Mom asked.

"They're cool enough now. Look how easily they come out of their molds, Harriet," Carolyn noticed.

"Let's not break a one. We'll be careful. That will please Mom." When cooled, the candy sprang easily out of their molds with a gentle push on the underside of the pliable, rubber material.

My sisters and I carefully and patiently filled the boxes with fudge or maple leaves. First, a layer of waxed paper, which had been cut to exact size by Raymond a day or two before, was placed inside the box. Then the sweet treats were set carefully inside one by one, another layer of waxed paper, more goodies, and finally more paper was placed on top. The box and its contents were weighed on our small scale. When a pound was determined, the lid was folded over covering the box.

"Carolyn, here's the list of orders. Please write each address on the labels. I'll fill the boxes with the little kids' help," Mom said.

"All right, that's easy enough. Can I put on the stickers? Please Mom, I want to put on the stickers!"

"Wait, Sandy. Don't forget that the boxes need to be weighed before we seal them," Mom reminded her. An oval-shaped sticker held the top flap in place. Gold in color, each read *Pure Vermont Maple Products.*

Ray called Mom's candies "sweets for the senses."

Maple sugar can used today

"I'll weigh each box for you, and then Sandy can put on the stickers," Harriet suggested.

"And, I'll stack the filled boxes on the shelf."

"Okay, Pat you do that part. As soon as we finish this, I have my schoolwork to do. I have a lot to do," Harriet sighed.

The maple cream was poured into little round, shiny tin cans holding just a pound. Mom weighed every filled tin on her small scale to be certain of its weight. "Our customers get what they pay for. We don't shortchange anybody." Like Dad, Mom was honest.

Then each lid was pressed on tightly. Our family label was secured to it.

We had finished packing each box and labeling each tin. Now, Carolyn and Mom worked side by side, filling mailing boxes with combinations of maple fudge, maple spread, maple leaves, or cans of maple syrup.

"I'll tape down each box, and Carolyn, put your address label on each one as we go along. We don't want any mixed up orders this year."

"Right, Mom. No mistakes this year. I guarantee!" said Carolyn with a laugh.

Within a few minutes, Mom declared, "There. The orders are done until we start another round of orders that arrived in today's mail. Carolyn, can you get the baked goods out of the pantry and the cards you kids have made for Gene? We'll pack his box."

Early the next morning, Dad carried the packages to the car to make another trip to the post office with the sweet, heavy bundles. "Hey, what's in this box for Gene? It's as heavy as a box of rocks!"

"I always send him plenty. Gene wrote that some guys never hear from home. When his buddies find out that he has received another box, they crowd around him for samples," Mom laughed.

Over time, Mom had learned that her customers wanted every maple leaf perfect and every piece of fudge uniform in size. Small pieces, broken, or misshapen candies were set aside and kept on a plate along with the occasional broken pieces of the leaf-shaped treats. Sometimes, when Mom cut the fudge, the pieces were too small. Corner pieces were not sold. They were on the plate, too.

Eagerly, my sisters and I, Raymond, Clarence, and Gene before he left home, ate the broken candies, never tiring of the sweet taste. At breakfast, as we spread maple cream on our toast, Dad expressed his pride in our mother.

"How your mother cleans this house, does all the shopping, cooks for us every day, and has time to earn extra money is beyond me. Raymond is spending so much time working with the Bigelows that he has precious little time to help in this kitchen anymore."

Our maple products were a cash crop and the profits had a special use. "Let's see, this year we need Christmas cards and postage stamps, tinsel for the tree, and replacements for the bubble lights. Oh, let's add wrapping paper. The paper we've saved from year to year has been used once too often." Mom was making a long list.

She purchased what she called house gifts, items that were used by everyone. "We need new towels, some nice soap for you girls, and some real glasses for the table. I've grown tired of the old and nicked metal tumblers. You kids are old enough now to be careful not to drop a glass. If you girls would like anything special this year, add it to my list."

"I'm going to ask for a paint-by-number set, Sandy."

"Oh, Patty, me too. I want dancing ballerinas standing

Shipping label for the Chase maple products from the 1950s

on their tippy toes. Which one do you want?"

"Belmain's Store has a set with ships out on the ocean. That's what I want. I also want a Girl Scout pin."

Later, in the evening, I heard Dad and Mom talking. "Now, Mary, you buy something just for you. You could use a new dress and apron."

"I'm planning to use any leftover money for a new fedora and a frock for you," Mom answered cheerfully.

"The frock and fedora have a lot of use left in them. My barn coat and old hat are just fine. They're fine."

Mom smiled at him and raised her eyebrows.

Chapter 31

WORKING FOR THE STATE OF VERMONT

It seems to me that the tradition of respect for work is so ingrained in this country that it is not surprising fathers have handed it down to their daughters as well as their sons.
Eleanor Roosevelt

School was out for the summer. Our crops were planted and growing. Uncle Jim delivered the mail as usual on that warm June day. He handed the day's stack to Harriet.

"I think I have what you girls have been waiting for."

It seemed as if we had waited forever, but sure enough, the Social Security cards were in the mail's pile. My sisters and I quickly opened our letters.

"Here's one of Dad's pens. We need to sign our card." Carolyn wrote her name and passed the pen around.

"I'll get our job applications out of Dad's desk."

I ran through the living room and returned with the applications. We took turns and each wrote our number, nine digits in all, on the application papers.

"Your number is important and you need to remember them. If anyone asks you, you'll have it on the tip of your tongue. And keep that card in a safe place. You'll need it anywhere you work in this country," Dad told us.

We piled into the car and Mom drove us to the VSA. Excited, we arrived with the applications in our hands.

Mr. Lavalle, the groundsman, was happy to see us.

"Mrs. Young has been waiting for these papers. I will give them to her right now. Be here tomorrow morning at eight a.m."

"All right," answered Harriet. "That's time enough to call in the cows and to feed our calves and pigs. We'll have just time enough for a quick breakfast just as we do for school." We all nodded.

And so on the very next day, right after wolfing down breakfast, we four girls bypassed the road and hurried off through our fields and Mr. Brigham's apple orchard. Within a few minutes we arrived. Janice, who was the daughter of the school principal and Harriet's friend and classmate, met us. Janice and her parents had helped us get our first job.

It was nearly eight o'clock. "We can walk over to the fields where Mr. Lavalle is waiting." Janice pointed in the direction of a large garden.

"Let's hurry!" Sandy and I motioned to Janice.

Mr. Lavalle waited by a pickup truck loaded with many, many quart-sized wooden baskets and big wire carrying trays.

Mr. Lavalle explained our responsibilities. "For the next few days, if the weather stays sunny and warm, you'll pick strawberries. Pick only the red strawberries."

Well, that's easy I thought to myself. For years, Sandy and I have picked the wild strawberries that grew along our meadows and near our meandering brook. If Ray was lucky, we had a few berries for him to add to his rhubarb pies.

Mr. Lavalle continued, "Leave the whitish or pinkish ones. They'll ripen within a day or two because it is so hot and sunny. Never select any spoiled berry. Leave them where they are."

Poking Sandy, I whispered, "Does he think we've never seen a red strawberry?"

"He thinks this is our first day on a farm." Sandy and I giggled childishly. Carolyn and Harriet frowned for they were serious and Janice, too. Mr. Lavalle handed us a stack of wooden baskets and assigned us our rows.

Those tiny wild strawberries were miniatures compared to the strawberries we now picked from the cultivated beds at the VSA. Wow! It took so little time to fill the bottom of a quart-sized basket. Immediately, the basket's bottom was covered and almost as quickly the basket was full. And then another! And still another! My enthusiasm for the task increased. These strawberries were big! They were juicy and tasty!

"Try some," I urged Sandy.

Together we gobbled up many of the red, juicy berries. Harriet, Carolyn, and Janice had more willpower and ate none while we worked.

"Each one is a mouthful," I murmured to Sandy as one juicy berry after another filled my mouth. Juice trickled down my chin.

"Now, Pat, don't talk with a full mouth. Be polite."

Mr. Lavalle gathered up our full baskets. Carrier after carrier was filled and placed in the back of the truck one flat stacked on another. The stacks steadily grew.

"You're all doing a good job. That is enough picking for today. I'll drive these containers to the kitchen. That's where the real work begins. Follow the truck."

When we arrived, we carried the strawberries into the kitchen where we met Mrs. Lavalle.

"Oh, look at the berries you girls have gotten. You have so many!" Mrs. Lavalle smiled and handed each of us a glass of water. After two hours in the hot sun, we were thirsty.

"Wash your hands and use soap!" Mrs. Lavalle showed us the bathroom. Then she showed us the jobs that needed to be done.

First, Mrs. Lavalle used a large colander and rinsed one quart at a time. Next, the berries were hulled to remove the stems. Third, we cut the berries into two or three slices.

"You can tell by eyeing the berry how many slices to make." Mrs. Lavalle showed us.

We each used a small knife and wooden cutting board. There were bowls all around to fill with sliced berries.

As we worked, Mrs. Lavalle continued rinsing the berries and added them to more bowls. She emptied our filled ones into a huge stainless steel bowl. We grabbed another bowl of the rinsed berries and sliced them. Mrs. Lavalle measured the amount of berries as she went along. She added sugar and stirred until the berries were juicy. They turned redder and juicier by the minute. Yum.

I eyed Sandy with an expression that said, "Yummy!" Sandy laughed and blurted out, "These berries look good enough to eat!"

Mrs. Lavalle stopped stirring and smiled. "It's time for a rest. Let's enjoy a dish of strawberries. Come sit at the table. Bring your water glasses, girls. Oh, my how you Chase girls can work! You, too, Janice," she said. Mrs. Lavalle appreciated a job well done.

"Isn't anybody in here working today?" Mr. Lavalle asked when he returned to the kitchen. He filled his old coffee cup with water and helped himself to a bowl of berries.

We returned to work with one of us rinsing, others hulling, and two others slicing. Mrs. Lavalle brought out stacks of quart-sized white, cylindrical containers from another cupboard and filled each one with the sweetened berries. Because everyone knew Carolyn was neat, she wrote on each lid: "Fresh Strawberries, 1954, VSA."

Mrs. Lavalle showed Harriet where to stack the containers in the freezer. When my turn came to go into the freezer, I was astonished. WOW! I could walk right into it!

I had never seen such an enormous freezer. There were big tubs of Hood ice cream, a few packages of frozen vegetables, loaves of bread, and frozen meats. It was nice and cold and my arms felt good because the kitchen had grown hotter by the minute.

I whispered to myself, "This is neat!"

We worked all morning at one job or another processing the berries. After five hours, the berries had been picked, rinsed, hulled, sliced, stirred with sugar, placed in containers with tight lids, identified with Carolyn's handiwork, and carried to the freezer.

"The Aggies will enjoy fresh frozen strawberries all winter long. I'll serve strawberry shortcake several times and strawberries with ice cream for the students." Mrs. Lavalle sounded proud of her work.

We walked to Janice's house on the campus. My stomach growled. The strawberries had not satisfied my hunger. Mrs. Young met us at the door.

"Come in, girls. Tomorrow bring a lunch, whatever you take with you for a school lunch. You will work more hours tomorrow. Today you have each worked five hours."

I watched her write the hours on a piece of paper. Beside our names, she had written our Social Security numbers. Five hours of work!

"Please check to be sure your Social Security number is accurate." Mrs. Young passed the paper around.

After inspecting my number, I said, "My Social Security number is correct." My three sisters agreed as they checked their number. Dad had been right. We needed to recall our number when needed.

Sandy and I figured out the total amount we had earned as we walked home. At seventy five cents per hour, our earnings totaled three dollars and seventy five cents.

"Wow!" exclaimed Sandy. "Patty, that's more than we earn during a whole month except for the potato and sugaring season."

"Yup! We're lucky to be paid minimum wage. Little kids don't have to be paid the right amount of money. We're lucky. And farm people don't have to be paid that either."

We arrived home, tired and hungry. Lassie announced our arrival, barking, wagging her tail, and racing up the path to greet us. She sniffed my hand as I petted her.

"You're a good dog, Lassie," I murmured as she licked my fingers which were sticky with strawberry juice and sugar.

"We need lunches for tomorrow, Raymee," Sandy mentioned as she and the rest of us wolfed down Raymond's latest cooking idea, a cake with a delicious fudge-like pudding on top. It was a chocolaty delight.

"Hey! Save some of that for dessert tonight!" Make your own sandwiches. You can make egg salad sandwiches. If you can boil water, you're all set. I'm not your slave."

"I'm making a peanut butter and jelly sandwich."

"Me, too, if you'll let us in the kitchen," piped up Sandy.

Raymond asked many questions about our job. When he was satisfied with our details, he continued, "Who would hire you little kids? Who'd pay you money? I can't believe you're paid the same as Harriet and Carolyn. They know how to work. That school must be desperate for help. Both of you are such weaklings!"

Mom gave him a look that seemed to say, "Leave the little kids alone, Raymond."

Sandy and I had grown accustomed to Raymond's teasing. We complained about him to Dad or Mom. Dad often responded to our complaints with, "Learn to let sleeping dogs lie. Your brother's not dangerous. He's just letting off steam in his own way. He's searching for himself."

Once Sandy had said, "He'll know where he is when I punch him!"

"Now, Sandy, don't get yourself all worked up and upset," Dad had cautioned.

After lunch, we skipped through the fields to deliver Dad's lunch. We carried sandwiches and switchel, an old-fashioned drink consisting of ginger, Grade B syrup, vinegar, and water.

"There he is, over there!" exclaimed Sandy as she broke into a run.

Dad was checking the young potato plants. If he saw any evidence of fungus, he'd take out the sprayer. "I'll nip

Sandy, age 9

it in the bud," he said. Lassie led the way, happy to see Dad, too. Both Sandy and I had a lot to tell him about our first real job!

"Hello, Daddy!" Sandy shouted. "We're back and we have to work tomorrow, too." She ran ahead of me.

Dad paused, waved, stood straight, and tall. When we reached him, he took a long drink of switchel. "So, how did you like picking strawberries today?" he grinned.

"We have to go to work tomorrow, too."

"So now you're all grown up with your first job that pays you by the hour."

Chapter 32

THAT FIRST JOB

You're always learning something. Because I'm older doesn't
mean that I've stopped learning. You'll see. There's something
to learn every day if you pay attention.
My father, Raymond E. Chase

That first "real job" of harvesting and processing strawberries lasted four days. My sisters and I had worked a
total of twenty hours. We earned seventy five cents per
hour. That was fifteen dollars. A little of that wage automatically was sent by our employer, the State of Vermont, to the federal government's Social Security fund.
I now owned a Social Security card that gave me, as
with anyone else who had one, the ability to retire with
monthly payments beginning at age sixty-five.

"When you're that old, Patty, you'll be reading in your
rocking chair and enjoying all the money you receive
every month," Sandy kidded.

"Yes, and you'll be a grandmother, and your grand-
children will sit on your lap and listen to stories about
working so hard in the hot sun to earn your retirement
money."

"I'll tell them about our trip to the World's Fair in Tunbridge, Vermont! They will want to go there, too."

"The fair has been going on for almost a hundred

years. How long do you think the fair will continue?" I asked.

"The fair will last just as long as Dad's cedar shingles on the barn. And that's until time wears them away!"

At the bank, my sisters and I each cashed our paycheck remembering to write our signature on the reverse side. We deposited most of the money into our accounts. We each kept a little for our immediate needs: money for magazines, comics, movie tickets, popcorn, and, of course, candy.

***

Now as an adult I look back at my childhood. I often think about the tasks we accomplished, the problems we faced, the dangers we dodged, and the fun we experienced at work and play.

Did these activities foster an industrious attitude and cooperation among my siblings? Of course. Did these activities lead to independence? Most definitely. Had such activities created in each of us a sense of self-reliance? Certainly. Had these jobs around the farm fostered a sense of teamwork? That goes without saying. Did these various tasks develop a strong work ethic? Without a doubt.

My siblings and I were children. There were times when I wanted to be more of a child. I wanted more time to play with my dog, Lassie. I longed for more free time to ride my bike on the country roads near our farm, pumping the pedals with busy legs to struggle up a steep hill and then fly effortlessly down the other side.

Without responsibilities, Sandy and I no doubt could have had more playful adventures during our growing years. In the springtime, Sandy and I liked to walk the short distance from our home to the small pond and listen to the peepers and hear the bullfrogs rib-bit, rib-bit. There, we selected more than our share of pussy willows for Mom and for the teachers at school. We liked to watch the red-winged blackbirds as they flew about as decoys to keep human intruders from straying too close to their nests among the cattails.

During summer evenings, just as darkness approached, we caught fireflies and placed them in jars with well-ventilated covers. The fireflies became tiny lanterns in darkened bedrooms.

We built a little hut nestled among the maples near our garden. It was a primitive structure to be sure but one that brought us much pleasure. Clarence offered his services but this was a project we wanted to do by ourselves. And although we never thanked him for the nails, screws, rope, and tools from his toolbox, we appreciated his advice, which we frequently needed.

We would sit inside our curtained structure and while away the time telling each other silly stories, discussing school friends, school activities, and sharing our reading materials. We wrote to our pen pals from the hut.

We giggled as we told each other silly, silly jokes. What color is a blue jay? What are the colors of a red-winged blackbird? What is black and white and red (read) all over? Knock knock jokes were popular back then. Pete and Repeat jokes were a hoot. Silly, yes, but fun.

More time to read favorite books would have been wonderful. Although Sandy knew how to read, she liked to be read to from my favorites.

On hot summer days, we kids often walked through the pasture to the brook's cool water near the pasture's end. When Gene had been home, he had dammed up the brook with rocks and clay making the wading area waist deep. That was close to heaven on a hot day! Even the cows enjoyed standing in the cool water covering their udders and underbellies as they swatted away nasty flies with bushy tails.

I wanted to skip rope with my friends as I had done during school time. I longed to play more with those kittens in the barn that I tamed and seduced with warm milk. Sandy and I, with Lassie by our side, yearned to visit friends just a short walk down the road to play dodge ball or hide and seek, swing on their swing set, relax on their lawn, talk about school, and enjoy a summer breeze on a hot day. I think all of my siblings yearned for leisure.

There are memories I wouldn't give up for the world. The satisfaction of completing a task you could easily observe is rewarding. The warm feeling of being com-plimented for the completion of a chore warmed our hearts. Working, or tagging along with Sandy by my side, as Clarence or Dad labored around our farm, is a priceless memory.

In many ways our work was play. The delight of part-nering together with my siblings to complete our chores is a memory of childhood and one of a lasting bond and affection. Our farm animals, the cows, the calves and the pigs, too, were our friends.

Remember, "Enjoy being little, we all start out that way," Dad was fond of saying.

EPILOGUE

Dost thou love life? Then do not squander time;
for that's the stuff life is made of.
Benjamin Franklin

More than fifty years have flown by since I began retracing my experiences on the family farm. One by one we kids left the farm except for Clarence who stayed to operate it with Dad. After Dad passed away in 1961, the farm was sold to the Guy Lake family who operated and lived there for over thirty years. Mom remarried in the early 1960s and moved to New Mexico where she passed away in 1977.

Aunt Almira Davis passed away in 1962 while I was in college. Her children, Myron Chapman and Mary Chapman, have both died, Myron in 2004 and Mary in 2005.

Clarence purchased his own farm in Tunbridge, Vermont. He continued to develop a registered Holstein herd. He died in 1973.

Dad's friend, James P. Wheatley, better known as Uncle Jim to the seven Chase children, died in 1970.

In 1997, the farm was registered with the Vermont Land Trust by the Lake family. That meant that the buildings and farmland would be used only for agricultural purposes, and would never be open to commercial or residential development.

Chase dairy barn with milkhouse on the left in the 1950s

Gene remained in California, married, and raised a family of four children. Gene worked for an advertising firm as a salesman and manager. He died in 2004. Raymond moved to California, too, after being part of the Army National Guard. He remained single and died in 1984. He had worked as a baker for a restaurant chain and soon became manager of the chain, the Salt Shaker Restaurants.

Harriet married and is the mother of seven sons. When they were grown, she returned to college, graduated, and worked as a vocational counselor. After living in many areas of our country, she decided to return to Randolph, Vermont, a few years ago. She is the volunteer curator of Randolph's Historical Museum and enjoys her retirement years and loves the task of promoting Randolph's history through the museum.

Carolyn, a registered nurse and once a restaurant owner and caterer, married Winfield Tandy. They are the parents of two children, now adults. Until their retirement to Arizona, they lived in Essex Junction, Vermont.

Sandy married and is the mother of four daughters. When her children were grown, she attended college, graduated, and is employed in hospital administration. Her home is in Wolcott, Connecticut.

All of my many nieces and nephews are now adults and many have families of their own. They work as therapists, teachers, nurses, counselors, real estate appraisers, engineers, hearing specialists, computer experts, computer sales people, financial advisors, landscape managers, and caregivers to their many children. Two nephews have served in Iraq, Shem and Seth Webler, Harriet's sons. Shem served in Iraq itself in the medical field. Seth served from Qatar fulfilling supply orders for shipment to Iraq. Another generation is in process.

As for me, I attended college, graduated, and became an elementary and middle level schoolteacher spending most of my career in Colchester, Vermont. At one time, I was married. My children were those who passed through my classroom year after year.

The present owners of the farm are Brent and Regina Beidler who have one daughter. They have worked to see

Chase barn today now owned by the Beidler family

that the farm is certified organic and their milk products are shipped to Organic Valley along with nine other
farms in the Randolph area. When they purchased the
farm, it consisted of 145 acres. Parcels had been sold
from the original acreage that Dad had owned.

Many of the big maples that shaded the nearby roads
and provided sap for syrup have been cut down. The old
horse barn has been demolished. The dairy barn still
sports cedar shingles and the fields continue to feature
crops and forage for Holsteins. The house, although un-
dergoing renovation, is recognizable as the childhood
home of seven Chase children and their mom and dad,
Mary Downing Chase and Raymond Eugene Chase.

The old path that led to the Langevin farm is nearly

Current owners of the Chase farm, Brent and Regina Beidler

invisible. The Langevin farm is home to the Vermont Veterans Memorial Cemetery, a gift from Bernie and Lucille. The Langevin home has undergone extensive renovations. It is now owned by Vermont Technical College and the State of Vermont and is used for conferences, a gathering place for memorial services at the Veterans Cemetery, and perhaps, more important, serves as a reminder of the once stately home it was in 1802 when it was first built.

In my introductory chapter, I wrote that Sandy and I felt locked in place at nine and eleven years old. How wrong we were! The years have flown by. As the two little kids, we made our way around the farm, sometimes helping and sometimes being underfoot.

Each of my siblings struggled to cope with the loss of the family farm in their own individual way. The sale of the family farm is a bittersweet memory, for many of us thought Clarence its rightful heir. As for me, part of my heart rests with the surrounding landscape, the memory of my childhood family, our family dog, our tons of kittens to adore, the curly tailed Yorkshire pigs to admire, and cows to cherish. Bounding off for school, lunch pail in hand, climbing the steep hill, and arriving at one of America's gifts offered to its young are priceless memories.

Everyone has family memories. Mine are of the ever changing seasons and the tasks that needed to be accomplished. Rising early every late spring, summer, and autumn day to call in the cows is a pleasant memory. I feel the mist of those foggy mornings on my cheeks. Up early in the winter, to feed our dairy herd with the help of my siblings is another lasting memory. Working in the fields at planting, weeding, and harvesting time kept us in rhythm with the seasons. The sugaring season was akin to the roll of drums in a marching band, an exciting time.

Caring for our animals created a sense of purpose for us, for they needed our attention every day. They needed water, hay, grain, molasses, and a pat on their soft fur. A wet kiss on my hand offering grain to a favorite animal can nearly be re-experienced. The memory of the pigs, always seemingly pleased and happy with their food, is a nostalgic memory.

The Chase sisters - Sandy, Pat, Carolyn, and Harriet - in 2007. Photo by Sean Pinney.

After we attended our chores and upon arrival at our family kitchen, food always awaited us, as if by magic. It wasn't until I began to write my memoirs that I appreciated the awesome task that was Mom's. She never complained, and although she enjoyed Raymond's assistance, she held the responsibility for providing well-balanced, nutritious meals for the family, every day. Three times a day. Seven days a week.

My brothers have all passed away, Mom, Dad, Aunt Almira, and Uncle Jim, too. When my sisters and I get together, we speak of Dad's many words of wisdom through proverbs, heard so often as children. Those words provide the four of us and through us to the succeeding generations, a clear path to the future. Proverbs never die and memories linger in our hearts.

BIBLIOGRAPHY

Anderson, Lorraine, ed. *Sisters of the Earth*. New York: Random House, 2003.

Bartlett, John. *Bartlett's Familiar Quotations*. Boston, Mass.: Little, Brown & Co., 1980.

Bennett, William J., ed. *The Book of Virtues for Young People*. New York: Scholastic, 1998.

Chase, Harriet, and Ronald Sanford. *Randolph Vermont, 1777-1927*. Northfield, VT, 2006.

Cooley, Harry H. *Randolph, Vermont Historical Sketches*. Brooklyn, NY: Theo. Gaus, Ltd.,1979.

Cooley, Harry H. *Record and Memorial of the Citizens of Randolph Vermont*. 1962.

Cooke, Jim. "The Day Calvin Coolidge Said: 'Vermont Is a State I Love'." *Vermont Life*, Spring 2004, 10-14.

Daniel, Clifton, ed. *Chronicles of the 20th Century*. Mount Kisco, NY: Chronicle Publications, 1987.

Freeman, Criswell. *Wisdom Made in America*. Nashville, TN: Walnut Grove Press, 1995.

Ganeri, Anita. *The BFC Young Book of How Things Grow*. St. Albans, England: David Bennett Books, 1995.

Goodman, Lee Dana. *Vermont Saints and Sinners*. Shelburne, VT: New England Press, 1985.

Griswold, A. Whitney. *Farming and Democracy*. New Haven: Yale University Press, 1948

Hayward, Susan. *A Guide for the Advanced Soul.* Avalon Beach NW, Australia: In-Tune Books, 1985.

http//www.betterbee.com/resources/funfacts.html

Kennedy, Senator Edward M. *America, Back on Track.* New York: Penguin Books, 2006.

Kilgore Brown, Cindy. *Vermont Wildlife Viewing Guide.* Helena, MT: Falcon Publishing Company, 1994.

Lingelbach, Jenepher, and Lisa Purcell, eds. *Hands-On Nature.* Woodstock, VT: University Press of New England, 2000.

Rood, Ronald. *Ron Rood's Vermont, A Nature Guide.* Shelburne, VT: New England Press, 1988.

Sewell, Anna. *Black Beauty.* Racine, WI: Whitman Publishing Company, 1965.

Historical documents and photographs. Randolph Historical Society, Randolph, Vermont.